THE *very* BEST VISITORS GUIDE TO
BARBADOS

GW00597413

by **Peter Hingston**

Author's Acknowledgements   The collection of information necessary to produce a guidebook requires the co-operation of many individuals and organisations. To them my grateful thanks. In particular I would like to thank Charlotte Hingston and Jimmy Walker for many constructive suggestions and for improving my original text. In addition I would like to thank the following who all contributed in some way or other (in alphabetical order): the Barbados National Trust, the Barbados Statistical Service, the Barbados Tourism Authority, Richard Goddard, Jane Olivier Publicity, Stuart Ramsden, Mike Seale, Jill Sheppard, Chris and Susan Trew. A special thanks to Colin Hudson for his advice on flora and fauna. Finally, I would like to thank the many people and organisations who provided photographs (listed below) or vetted the text appropriate to themselves.

Cover Photograph   By Dick Scoones and reproduced with his kind permission. Dick's fine photographs can be seen in his postcards of Barbados and in his book "Portrait of an Island".

Picture Credits   Photographs on pages 13 and 14 and the illustrations on page 27 courtesy the Government Information Service of Barbados (GIS); page 20 provided by Wild Feathers; page 21 provided by Atlantis Submarine; page 24 provided by Jean Baulu; pages 26 (both photos), 38, 49, 52 (top), 62 (bottom), 64, 65 and 67 provided by the Barbados Tourism Authority; pages 29 (top), 60, 62 (top) and 74 by Felix Kerr; page 34 (both photos) provided by Jeremy Sisnett; page 40 (both photos) provided by the Jolly Roger; pages 44, 52 (bottom) and 72 (both) by Susan Trew; page 63 by Elisabeth Roachford; page 66 by Mike Seale; page 73 provided by Cave Shepherd & Co Ltd; page 75 by Stephen Mayers; page 80 (top) provided by Hotel Investors Ltd; page 80 (bottom) provided by The Plantation Restaurant. All other photographs by Peter and Charlotte Hingston. We are also grateful to the Barbados National Trust for permission to use the old photographs on pages 12 and 31 which are from the Edward Stoute Collection.

Drawings   The watercolour on page 19, the drawings on pages 83 and 84 and the frieze design on pages 15, 61, 71 and 85 are by Jill Walker and reproduced with her kind permission.

Folded Map of Barbados and Street Plan of Bridgetown   Copyright © 1993 by Best of Barbados Limited. Produced with kind permission of the Lands & Survey Department, Government of Barbados.

Published by Hingston Associates, Westlands, Tullibardine, Auchterarder, Perthshire PH3 1NJ, U.K. with the assistance of Best of Barbados Limited, Welches, St Thomas, Barbados.

Distributed in Barbados and the Caribbean by Best of Barbados Limited, tel: (809) 421-6900. Distributed in the U.K. and elsewhere world-wide by Hingston Associates, tel: (0)764 662058.

ISBN 0 906555 15 9   Book printed in Singapore.

FOREWORD

When I saw this guide book I was reminded of the author who said: "Whenever I feel the need for a good book I write one". I suspect Peter Hingston felt that way about a Barbados guide book and set about to produce the perfect one.

I confess to a life long fascination for guide books or books of any kind about Barbados and the Caribbean. It began with a childhood read of Raymond Savage's "Barbados", published in 1936. The author wrote in a prosaic, slightly lyrical and gently witty style of the 1930s, and many of his descriptions etched themselves in my impressionable mind. One phrase in particular has reflected my own continuing love for Barbados: "I have discovered the nearest place to perfection that I am ever likely to find in this sad world".

What do we expect of a guide book? One of my dictionaries defines it as designed to direct, show the way and determine direction or course of conduct; to instruct in the elements, to guide, manage or regulate. So it can give the basics or do a great deal more. To borrow a phrase from Alexander Pope, it can be "Guide, philosopher and friend". Savage took the role of friend, with only a bit of general information on how to get there and a comment on the excessive taxi fares – $1 from Bridgetown to Hastings. Others, like Patrick Leigh Fermor have been philosopher, while others have been encyclopaedic, running to several hundred pages.

But good things come in small packages, like this book and Barbados. And both contain the most astonishing variety and range of attractive offerings, tightly packed. Barbados now has two dozen paying sites and attractions and another two dozen worthy sites of interest across the island, all enthusiastically (and accurately) summarised in "The *Very* Best Visitors Guide to Barbados", much of fascination in Bridgetown, and nearly two dozen craft shops around the island. The richness of the attractions is almost understated, as if the author didn't want to sway the reader too much into seeing his favourite places! He does highlight the excellent Barbados Heritage Passport (on page 16), which gives admission to many sites, from the unique Andromeda Botanical Gardens to a range of Sugar Plantation Great Houses. "The *Very* Best Visitors Guide to Barbados" by covering everything attractive to do or see, conveys the same message as the Heritage Passport, that there is an astonishing natural and man-made heritage to be discovered at every turn in Barbados.

This book does seem to do what it promises. Everything is here, in 90 odd pages, from the ancient churches to the National Trust Sunday Hikes, from where to eat to how to cook it (by buying a good Caribbean recipe book!). It speaks to all sensitive and curious visitors, who we hope will take warm and wonderful memories and beautiful photos, and leave nothing but their footprints.

Professor Henry Fraser
President, Barbados National Trust

CONTENTS

MAP OF THE CARIBBEAN

SCALE

| 0 | 200 | 400 | 600 | 800 kilometres |

| 0 | 100 | 200 | 300 | 400 | 500 miles |

U.S.A.

Florida

Bermuda

The Bahamas

ATLANTIC OCEAN

Turks & Caicos Islands

CUBA

G R E A T E R

Hispaniola

Cayman Islands

Haiti

Dominican Republic

Puerto Rico

St Thomas

Tortola

Anguilla

St Martin

St Barthélemy

Virgin Is

Barbuda

Jamaica

A N T I L L E S

St Croix

St Kitts & Nevis

Antigua

Montserrat

Guadeloupe

CARIBBEAN SEA

Dominica

Martinique

L E S S E R   A N T I L L E S

LEEWARD & WINDWARD ISLANDS

St Lucia

St Vincent

BARBADOS

Grenadines

Aruba

Curacao

Bonaire

Grenada

Margarita

Tobago

Trinidad

PANAMA

Orinoco River

V E N E Z U E L A

G U Y A N A

C O L O M B I A

B R A Z I L

BARBADOS — AN INTRODUCTION

Geography

Barbados is a tropical island lying just north of 13° latitude and west of 59° longitude. The island's maximum length is 21 miles (34km) and its maximum width is just under 15 miles (24km) with an area of 166 square miles (430 sq km).

For such a small island the topography varies considerably and pleasantly surprises those who are new to Barbados. It varies from a plateau in the south to quite hilly, rugged terrain in the north east, appropriately called the Scotland district. The beaches vary too, from the tranquil Caribbean shores of the west and south-west to the wilder eastern coastline of the Atlantic Ocean.

The highest point on the island is Mount Hillaby at 1,116ft (340m). The island is predominantly coral, unlike its neighbours in the Lesser Antilles which are volcanic and much older. It is the coral which gives Barbados its beautiful white sandy beaches.

People

The warm welcome which Barbadians extend to visitors has helped to make the island a popular holiday destination.

There are about 260,000 people in Barbados, making it one of the most densely populated countries in the world. However, the bulk of the population lives in and around the capital, Bridgetown, or along the built-up west and south coasts. There is therefore plenty of countryside and space especially in the north and eastern areas of the island that are rural with scattered villages.

Most Barbadians ("Bajans") are of African descent, though there are a significant number of European, Indian and mixed-descent people. English is the language spoken with a Bajan dialect and there is a high standard of literacy. Schooling is compulsory to the age of 16, and there are colleges of further education and the University of the West Indies (UWI) at Cave Hill. The University has campuses in Jamaica, Trinidad and Barbados.

Most religions are well represented on the island and church-going is practised by many. The eleven parish churches are all Anglican as Barbados adopted the state religion of England when the island was a colony. Today about half the population are baptised as Anglicans.

Politics

Barbados is an independent state and a member of the Commonwealth and the United Nations. The country achieved its independence from Britain peacefully in 1966, after 339 years as a colony. Unlike its neighbouring islands, Barbados was always a British colony. Today, Queen Elizabeth II is Head of State and is represented on the island by the Governor-General, who is a Barbadian.

The country's political, judicial and administrative systems were originally based on those found in Britain. In Parliament, the Prime Minister presides over a Cabinet and there are two Chambers – the House of Assembly and the Senate. The House of Assembly has elected MPs (Members of Parliament) and elections have to be held at least every 5 years. The Senate comprises appointed Senators who are eminent Barbadians. In 1989, Barbados celebrated 350 years of parliamentary rule. Since Independence, politics have been dominated by two parties – the Barbados Labour Party (BLP) and the Democratic Labour Party (DLP), but more recently a third party, the NDP has been launched.

Climate

The climate is considered by many to be among the finest in the world. Barbados can boast of having 3,000 hours of sunshine each year, which equates to over 8 hours per day. The temperature remains remarkably constant between a daytime mean *maximum* of 86°F and a night-time mean *minimum* of 69°F (30°C and 21°C). Except for the sheltered city centre, the cool and steady north-east trade winds help to make Barbados a very pleasant environment.

Sunrise is about 5.30am, while the sudden and often spectacular sunset occurs just after 6pm. These times do not vary much year-round due to the island's proximity to the equator.

Visitors often ask when is the best time of year to visit the island. Being close to the equator, the weather here remains much the same all year, but February and March are usually the driest months and the island can get quite brown. From about July to November the island gets the most rain and the trade wind tends to be less, so it can feel slightly hotter and more humid. But an advantage of visiting the island at that time is the beautiful flowering trees (the flamboyant in particular) and the greenery.

Hurricanes can be a problem throughout the Caribbean region, from Trinidad in the south to Florida in the north. They tend to spawn well to the south-east of Barbados and as they pass over water they build up in strength. Luckily their northbound track usually misses Barbados. The last major hurricane to strike the island was in 1955. However, during the months of July to November there may be a few days of heavy tropical rain if a hurricane passes nearby on its way north.

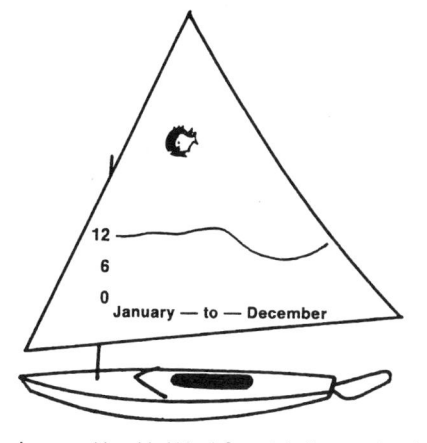

Average Monthly Wind Speed (miles per hour)

Economy

Within only a few decades of the first settlers arriving in 1627, sugar dominated the economy and this remained the case until the middle of this century. At times during this long period sugar reaped great profits for the plantation owners though at other times, due to many different causes, there have been large financial losses, which bankrupted many planters. Sugar production has fallen from post-war peaks of 200,000 tons to around 50,000 tons today.

Since World War II, the economy has diversified with manufacturing and tourism becoming more important. Computer-data input services has grown also. The island's manufacturing sector provides local and export markets with food and drink products (especially rum), garments, printing, electronics, furniture, hardware, medical supplies and building materials including cement from the giant Arawak cement plant.

Tourism is a key industry today with some 370,000 cruise line passengers visiting Barbados each year, together with around 400,000 longer stay visitors who arrive by air. There are just under 5,000 hotel/apartment bedrooms (excluding villas that can be rented) and standards range from self-catering apartments up to prestige international hotels. Estimated tourist expenditure is around one billion Barbados Dollars, which is almost 12% of the country's GDP (Gross Domestic Product).

The major trading partners of Barbados are the other members of CARICOM (Caribbean Common Market) with 16% of imports (31% of exports), Britain with 11% of imports (17% of exports), the USA with 33% of imports (12% of exports) and Canada with 6% of imports (3% of exports). There are also significant imports from Japan (motor vehicles) and Venezuela.

Since the 1960s, the Barbados Government has encouraged overseas companies to set up on the island with considerable fiscal incentives for appropriate companies such as manufacturers, offshore banks, Exempt Insurance Companies, Foreign Sales Corporations and International Business Companies. This is an area of the economy that the Government wishes to expand. For further information, contact the Barbados Investment & Development Corporation, tel: (809) 427-5350, fax: (809) 426-7802.

Communications

Barbados has excellent air links with other Caribbean islands, North America, Britain and parts of Europe. Its airport, named after Sir Grantley Adams (the island's first Premier), handles jumbo jets and Concorde. The large Deep Water Harbour, completed in 1961, serves not only cruise liners but also container ships. Smaller inter-island vessels as well as the *Jolly Roger* and *Bajan Queen* use the Shallow Draft harbour.

The telephone system on the island is to North American standards with features such as "call waiting" and "call forwarding" available as are mobile cellular phones. When phoning or faxing North America or Europe you will normally get a clear line due to the use of satellite links. Local calls on the island are usually free.

There is a high level of car ownership in Barbados and in the 1980s the many miles of paved (tarmac) roads were augmented by a new highway linking the airport to the west coast, skirting Bridgetown. The three sections of this new road were named after three eminent Barbadians – Prime Ministers Tom **A**dams and Errol **B**arrow and Premier Gordon **C**ummins, and so the road has become known as the ABC Highway.

Flora & Fauna

More than half the "greenery" seen by visitors was introduced by man. The relatively limited flora which arrived naturally came mainly from the Orinoco as rafts of floating vegetation, from nearby islands during hurricanes and by seeds adhering to the feet of migratory birds. Barbados has few endemic species of plants, but it is likely that the Grapefruit originated in Barbados as a natural cross between an Orange and a Shaddock. The national flower is the "Pride of Barbados".

Man was also responsible for the few species of wild animal on the island (in particular the mongoose, rat and monkey). But birds had little difficulty in coming. There are about two dozen species of birds that are normally resident though others winter on the island or migrate through. The birds you are most likely to see include the Blackbird (Grackle), Sparrow, Yellow Breast and Wood Dove. The charming Hummingbird is common in gardens. In rural areas the Cattle Egret is quite numerous and can often be seen heading back to Graeme Hall Swamp at dusk. And it is at dusk that you hear the vocal but tiny whistling frogs and crickets everywhere. Although nocturnal you may also see Giant Toads.

There are two species of snake (both harmless) – a tiny blind one that is mentioned in the Guinness Book of Records as being the shortest in the world (under 4¼ inches, 108mm) and a grass snake. The absence of other snakes is probably due to the introduction of the mongoose to reduce the damage done to sugar-cane by rats ■

BARBADOS — A BRIEF HISTORY

The First Settlers

Prior to the European settlers, the island was inhabited at various times by tribes from South America. These Amerindians from the Orinoco area had paddled north and settled on most of the Caribbean islands. It is not known exactly when they first landed on Barbados or even when they finally departed, but from artifacts it appears that they had arrived by the 7th century or even earlier and they had all gone by the mid 16th century.

Most relics belong to the Arawaks, who were probably the last inhabitants before the English. The Arawaks fished and farmed and lived mainly around the coast. Some of their artifacts can be seen today in the Barbados Museum. There are a number of theories as to why they left the island after so many centuries. It was once thought that the warlike and cannibalistic Caribs replaced the Arawaks, but only Arawak sites have been found in Barbados. Carib raids may have been only a contributory factor in depopulating the island. A more probable cause dates from the decisions in 1511 and 1512 by the Spanish to enslave people in the region to work their mines in Hispaniola. They raided all the islands, including Barbados, and those frightened Arawaks they missed probably paddled back to the relative safety of the Orinoco from where their ancestors had come.

Discovery By Europeans

Nobody can be sure which European first saw Barbados, but it certainly wasn't Christopher Columbus. He never sighted the island as he passed down the Leeward & Windward island chain. However, by the 1500s both the Spanish and Portuguese knew of the island's existence. The origins of the name "Barbados" are uncertain, though there are a number of theories, but we can be sure that the Spanish and Portuguese were referring to it as "Los Barbados" or something very similar from the early 1500s.

In 1625, Captain John Powell the elder, landed from his ship and claimed the island for "James, King of England". Powell's report encouraged his backer, Sir William Courteen, a leading London merchant, to finance the settlement of the island.

The New Colonists

In February 1627 the vessel *William and John* anchored off the west coast. There were less than a hundred settlers (including some captured slaves) on board. They landed at a place which is now known as Holetown.

They found the island uninhabited and relatively inhospitable, with forest and dense undergrowth covering the whole land down to the shore. There was little game apart from some pigs and few food-bearing plants. Captain Powell left the new settlers and departed for Brazil to find supplies. He returned with food and seed and a number of Arawaks who were to teach the settlers how to plant and grow the crops.

Shortly afterwards his brother, John Powell, arrived with two ships and more settlers. Unfortunately for the settlers and unknown to them, the new King (Charles I) had granted the "proprietorship" of the island to the Earl of Carlisle (after whom Carlisle Bay is named). The Earl had substantial debts and granted 10,000 acres of the island to a number of London merchants to whom he owed money. These merchants sent their own settlers under Governor Wolverston, and they arrived on the island in 1628 and settled in the area now known as Bridgetown. There was friction between the two rival groups but ultimately Carlisle's faction gained full control.

Colonisation progressed at a rapid rate and the population of the island, which had been less than one thousand for several years, reached 10,000 by 1640. Most of the settlers were young Englishmen. Besides subsistence crops, they grew cotton, tobacco and ginger for export. The quality of life for everyone was pretty basic, however.

The Arrival of Sugar

Then an event occurred that was to change the whole course of history for the island. In the late 1630s sugar-cane plants were brought from Brazil. Within a decade almost every sizeable arable plot on Barbados was given over to the growing of this valuable crop. Such was its importance that it became the currency of commerce. Even the Governor's salary was paid in sugar.

One of the first sugar planters was James Drax who, it is said, was also responsible for introducing windmills to the island for crushing sugar-cane. Prior to wind power, oxen mills had been used. In time there were hundreds of windmills in operation on the island until they were ultimately replaced by steam engines. (One windmill, Morgan Lewis, has been preserved – see the chapter BEST THINGS TO SEE & DO). James Drax made a fortune in sugar, owning Drax Hall, one of the largest plantations on the island. He was knighted, thus becoming the first Barbadian to be so honoured. Drax Hall is the only sugar plantation still in the original family's possession.

For virtually the next three centuries the sugar industry dominated every aspect of life in Barbados, at times making great profits for the few but resulting in slavery for the many. It was virtually the only industry on the island, with every other business being dependent upon it in one way or another.

By 1655 there were 745 sugar plantations and land values, not surprisingly, had risen dramatically. The economies of scale required to grow and process sugar meant that a plantation had to be at least 100 acres and preferably much more. This resulted in many of the early non-sugar smallholders selling out and moving to other islands or to America. In fact by the end of the 17th century the European population in Barbados had fallen to just over 20,000. In contrast, the negro slave population on the island had risen to over 40,000.

The Civil War in England and its impact on Barbados

In 1642 there was civil war in England with Parliament, under Oliver Cromwell, rebelling against King Charles I. Barbados managed to keep out of the trouble but an increasing number of defeated Royalists began to arrive on the island. After the King's execution in 1649 these Royalists proclaimed the Prince of Wales as the new King Charles II. They also managed to expel several prominent Barbadians, including Colonels Drax and Alleyne, who had supported Cromwell's Roundheads.

This was a bad decision by the Royalists as Drax and others reported these rebellious actions to the authorities in England. As a result, in 1651 a fleet with 4,000 men set out for Barbados from Plymouth. Colonels Drax and Alleyne accompanied the expedition under Sir George Ayscue. It resulted in a successful naval blockade followed by the Royalists accepting the authority of the English Parliament. The terms, known as the Charter of Barbados, gave Barbados the power to set its own taxes – an important step on its route to self-government.

In 1658 Cromwell died, but he left a legacy that was to have an important impact on the sugar trade – the much hated Navigation Acts. These forced all colonies to use only British merchant ships and not to trade directly with foreign countries. The price of sugar dropped steeply and many people in Barbados suffered.

Barbados' Military History

In 1665 when a Dutch fleet attacked Bridgetown, the cannon of Charles Fort, manned by the Barbados Militia, repelled the enemy. Today the remains of this fort can be found in the grounds of the Hilton Hotel. With continuing wars between the European nations who had colonies in the West Indies, the island's fortifications were steadily improved with ultimately a line of forts all along the west coast.

In 1778 France declared war on Britain and quickly captured Dominica, St Vincent and Grenada. Barbados was vulnerable, so in 1780 British troops arrived and in 1785 the island became the headquarters of a permanent garrison with responsibility for the Windward and Leeward islands. Work began on the construction of the Garrison that would eventually take several decades and result in a considerable amount of military building work near the major forts of Charles and St Ann's.

As the 19th century progressed the number of troops stationed on the island declined with the decreasing military threat and in 1905-1906 the last British soldiers left. In their one and a quarter centuries of maintaining a garrison on Barbados, the greatest threat to the soldiers was not death from military action but from hurricanes and disease.

Natural (& Other) Disasters

On the north-western side of the Garrison Savannah is a small monument to the 14 soldiers and one married woman killed in the great hurricane of 1831, which also killed around 1,500 civilians and left most of the island's buildings in ruins.

It had not been the first great hurricane to afflict the island for the early settlers had one in 1675 and in the hurricane of 1780 several thousand people were killed. The last hurricane to strike Barbados was in 1955, when Hurricane Janet caused much damage, killed 35 people and left many thousands temporarily homeless. But the worst natural disaster was the cholera outbreak in 1854 that killed about 20,000 people.

Broad Street (looking towards Nelson's Statue), c1900.

Bridgetown suffered from many disastrous fires, especially in the 17th and 18th centuries. More recently, many buildings in central Bridgetown have been rebuilt after fires.

The American Connection

In the early years, Barbados had many links with the new colonies in America. The governors of several American states, such as Massachusetts and South Carolina, were Barbadians. Between 1670 and the end of that century several thousand Barbadians emigrated to Virginia, South Carolina and other states. Some of these emigrants were second sons who would not inherit their father's sugar plantations in Barbados.

The only trip George Washington made outside America was to Barbados, as a young lad in 1751. When the colonies in America declared their independence from Britain in 1775, they received some support from the colonists in Barbados.

Slavery & Indentured Servants

The new sugar industry was hungry for labour and the slave trade could provide it. The dreadful conditions on board the ships carrying the slaves from Africa are well known. Once the slaves had landed in Barbados and been sold to a plantation they were looked after better, not normally for any humanitarian reason but because they had value and were vital to the proper operation of the plantation. Conditions were still very harsh with hard manual labour and severe punishments. The killing of a slave was not even regarded as murder until 1805.

In Britain, by the end of the 18th century, there were considerable moves afoot to abolish slavery. However, the outbreak of war with France in 1792 caused a delay and it was not until 1833 that the Emancipation Act was passed in Britain and came into force in 1834. Complete freedom followed in 1838 after a period of so-called "apprenticeship" in most colonies.

Not surprisingly there had been a number of attempts by slaves to rebel against the system. The only armed revolt was that in 1816. It involved several thousand slaves and lasted four days before being crushed by the authorities. One of the principal leaders who died in the uprising was a slave named Bussa.

Karl Broodhagen's statue "Slave in Revolt", which is mounted in the middle of a roundabout on the ABC Highway, commemorates the 150th anniversary of emancipation and is known by many as the "Bussa Statue".

Working alongside slaves in the sugar-cane fields were indentured servants, known as "Redlegs", whose living conditions were often worse than those of the slaves. These indentured servants included large numbers of ordinary English men and women searching for a better life, as well as Cromwell's prisoners-of-war. The latter, including 400 Monmouth rebels, were deported to Barbados and sold to plantation owners. By the end of the century this movement had ceased.

Towards the 20th Century & Independence

At the time of slave emancipation, a remarkable man, Samuel Jackson Prescod, was becoming increasingly active in representing the free coloureds. He edited their first newspaper *The New Times*, later *The Liberal*, and then in 1843 become the first coloured man to be elected to the House of Assembly. He is honoured today with his portrait appearing on the Bds$20 note and the Polytechnic is named after him. Prescod was followed by other able coloured men, such as Conrad Reeves, who was also elected to the House of Assembly and ultimately became Chief Justice in 1886.

Slowly the democratisation of the island continued. In 1924 Charles Duncan O'Neal founded the Democratic League and in 1932 he was elected to the House of Assembly. Today his portrait appears on the Bds$10 note and one of the bridges in Bridgetown is named after him.

In 1934 another great name in the history of Barbados, Grantley Adams *(right)* was elected to the House of Assembly. He played a key role at the time of the riots in 1937 which ultimately resulted

Sir Grantley Adams, the first Premier.

in Britain considerably increasing its expenditure on the island. He was Vice-President of the newly founded Barbados Labour Party and President of the Barbados Workers Union. In 1954 he became the first Premier of the country and this marked the start of complete self-government for all domestic matters. He was knighted in 1957 and today the Bds$100 note bears his portrait and the Airport is named after him.

The number of people entitled to vote increased very slowly. In 1831 free coloureds were given the vote for the first time, in 1884 the vote was extended, but as there was still a property requirement there were fewer than 1% registered to vote. In 1943 the property qualification was reduced further and women were entitled to vote for the first time. Universal adult suffrage was introduced in 1950 and in 1962 the voting age was reduced from 21 to the present 18 years.

Following the collapse of the ill-fated Federation of the West Indies in 1962, the country moved forward to its own independence in 1966 when Errol W. Barrow *(right)* became the first Prime Minister of the newly independent nation. His government was defeated by J.M.G.M. "Tom" Adams (Sir Grantley Adams' son) in the 1976 election, but he returned to power after the 1986 election and remained Prime Minister until his death, in 1987. Errol Barrow's portrait appears on the Bds$50 note and a section of the ABC Highway is named after him. Sadly, both Adams and Barrow died whilst in office.

Errol W. Barrow,
the first Prime Minister

Barbados Today

Since independence in 1966, the country has achieved a greater degree of growth and a significant improvement in the living standards of the majority of its citizens. Many new buildings have been erected, new highways link the modern airport to the capital and the tourist industry has been developed. There is free education and health care for all and the range of consumer goods in the shops is the envy of many other small nations■

HISTORICAL MISCELLANY

1882-3	The Telephone introduced to Barbados, only 3 years after its introduction to London.
1905	Island celebrated 300th anniversary of first landing – but unfortunately the date was wrong!
1913	First aeroplane to fly in Barbados (but had to be brought in by ship).
1930	First Cricket Test Match held in Barbados.
1959	Balloon *Small World* arrived after crossing the Atlantic, last part with gondola acting as a boat.
1963	Barbados entered the space race when H.A.R.P. (High Altitude Rocket Programme) set up using two converted naval guns that fired projectiles high into space.
1970	Thor Heyerdahl's *Rall* raft made landfall in Barbados after crossing the Atlantic.
1975	Cricketer Sir Garfield Sobers knighted in a rare historical public ceremony.
1991	England managed to break West Indies Cricket Team's unbroken wins since 1973.

For a fascinating account of the country's early history, read Peter Campbell's book "Some Early Barbadian History". The Redlegs' interesting history is covered in Jill Sheppard's book "The Redlegs of Barbados".

THINGS TO SEE AND DO

Chapters in this Section:

Jill Walker

NOTES ON "BEST THINGS TO SEE & DO"

Opening Times If your schedule is tight and you are planning to visit somewhere near to its closing time, it would be prudent to phone first and check just when they plan to close that day. Note that some visitor attractions are closed on Public Holidays (which are listed in GENERAL INFORMATION A-Z at the end of this book).

Entrance Fees Although prices were correct at time of writing, some will rise during the year. We have quoted all Entrance Fees in Barbados Dollars.

Telephone Numbers If phoning from overseas, the area code for Barbados is 809. For instance, if phoning the Barbados National Trust Headquarters from the UK, then the whole number would be: 0101 809 426-2421.

Corrections & Comments We would appreciate information from any reader should you find details of the attractions listed in this section have changed or you have other comments. Please write to the author, Peter Hingston, c/o Best of Barbados Limited, Welches, St Thomas, Barbados. Fax: (809) 421-6393. Visitors from the UK may prefer to write to the author c/o Hingston Associates, Westlands House, Tullibardine, Auchterarder, Perthshire PH3 1NJ. We will always try to acknowledge your letter or fax, but please appreciate we may not be able to reply immediately.

THE BARBADOS HERITAGE PASSPORT

This is an ideal place to introduce the Heritage Passport, a small booklet, costing Bds$65, that gives you admission to all the National Trust properties plus: the Barbados Museum, Barbados Zoo Park & Oughterson House, the Bridgetown Synagogue, Codrington College, Francia Plantation House, Grenade Hall Forest & Signal Station, Harrison's Cave, the Mount Gay Rum Visitor Centre, St Nicholas Abbey, Sunbury Plantation House and Villa Nova. Children (under 12) are admitted free if accompanied by a Heritage Passport holder. In addition, the Atlantis Submarine and other advertisers will give a discount.

The Heritage Passport is produced by the Barbados National Trust, the heritage organisation of the nation, dedicated to the preservation of places of historic and architectural interest or natural beauty. The Heritage Passport is widely available from: any National Trust property, many of the other attractions listed in this book, several car rental firms, travel agents, the Barbados Tourism Authority (addresses on page 87) and the Barbados National Trust itself at Ronald Tree House, 10th Ave., Belleville, St Michael, Barbados. Tel: 426-2421 or 436-9033. Fax: 429-9055. (Note: There is also a Mini Passport of 5 properties that costs Bds$24).

ANDROMEDA BOTANICAL GARDENS

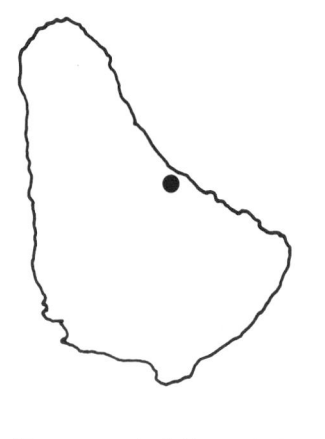

A corner of these delightful gardens with the Atlantic beyond.

These wonderful botanical gardens are the creation of the late Mrs Iris Bannochie who started them in 1954 for her own pleasure. Over the years the gardens grew in size (they cover nearly 8 acres today) and they became increasingly well-known internationally. They have been opened to the public on a regular basis since 1968.

The gardens follow the bed of an ancient stream with large coralstone boulders that inspired the name – in Greek mythology Andromeda was a maiden chained to a boulder as a sacrifice (happily she was rescued). The stream, which in rare times of heavy rain can become a raging torrent, attracted some of the original Arawak settlers and many of their artifacts have been unearthed in the gardens.

The gardens enjoy cooling sea breezes and there are shady areas under the trees with views of the Atlantic Ocean. Andromeda is arranged in individual gardens of tropical plants such as grafted hibiscus, orchids, bougainvillaea, cacti and palms. Thousands of plants have been introduced from around the world including many rare species. These plants were collected by Iris Bannochie and her husband, John, during extensive travels in North and South America, Europe and the Far East. The plants are numbered and a free leaflet describes each in detail.

On her death in 1988, Mrs Bannochie bequeathed Andromeda Gardens to the Barbados National Trust on the death of her husband. In the meantime it is leased to and managed by the Trust. Mrs Bannochie was well known in local and international horticultural circles, repeatedly helping to win awards for the Barbados Horticultural Society at the Chelsea Flower Show and other international flower shows. In 1977 she was honoured by the Royal Horticultural Society and in 1980 received the Silver Crown of Merit in the Barbados Honours List.

Open: *Daily (including week-ends), 9am–5pm.*
Time to allow: *1-2 hours.*
Facilities: *Best of Barbados gift shop. Toilets. The Hibiscus Café.*
Note: *Many paths not suitable for baby pushchairs or wheelchairs.*
Entrance Fee: *Bds$10. Children (under 12) and Seniors, half price.*
Telephone: *433-9261*

ANIMAL FLOWER CAVE & ARCHER'S BAY

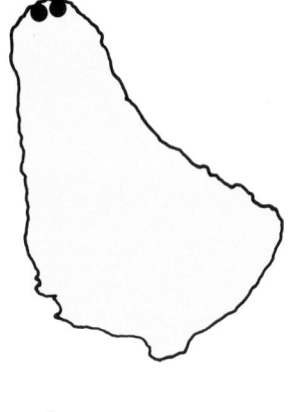

The Atlantic pounds the craggy northern coastline near the Animal Flower Cave.

"Animal flowers" is a local name for sea anemones which, tides permitting, can be seen in some of the caves. Located near the extreme northernmost point of the island, the Animal Flower Cave and surrounding cliffs make an interesting spectacle, especially when the waves are pounding on the cliffs throwing huge fountains of water 50-60ft (20m) upwards.

Descent into the caves is by a short but steep flight of stone steps. The entrance fee includes a tour guide and with his help you can easily enter a number of the caves. They are formed by the action of sea water, and you can look through the mouths of the caves to the ocean beyond.

Open: *Daily (including week-ends), 9am–5pm.*
Time to allow: *½ hour minimum.*
Facilities: *Refreshments.*
Entrance Fee: *Bds$4. Children (under 12) half price.*
Telephone: *439-8797*

Archer's Bay   A short distance to the west is Archer's Bay. Access by car to the cliff top is bumpy but there is some shade and the place is popular with locals as a picnic spot at week-ends and public holidays. There is a small beach but swimming here is not recommended.

Archer's Bay, in the northern-most parish of St Lucy.

ARTS & CRAFTS

There are a number of talented artists and crafts people working in Barbados. In some cases you can visit their studios and see them at work. Locally made goods include prints and screen-printed goods, pottery, batik, jewellery, leather goods, baskets, shell decorations and wood carvings. (See also the chapter on SHOPPING).

Charming watercolour by Jill Walker.

Best of Barbados These shops will give you an idea of the high quality of arts and craft gift items available on the island. Everything sold is made or designed in Barbados. The work of many Barbadian crafts people is represented, but the shops' main attraction is the work of artist and designer, Jill Walker. Jill's colourful tropical designs appear on trays, table mats, coasters, prints, games, mugs, a huge range of screen-printed items, cards, books...etc.

Best of Barbados shops are located at: Andromeda Botanical Gardens, Flower Forest, Mall 34 (Broad Street), Passenger Terminal (for cruise ships), Sam Lord's Castle, Sandpiper Inn (Holetown), Southern Palms Hotel (St Lawrence) and the Quayside Centre (Rockley). Open: Monday to Saturday, 9am–5pm (except Mall 34 which closes on Saturdays at 1pm and some shops are open on Sundays). Tel (Headquarters): 421-6900.

Castle Pottery (Castle, St Peter) This is a very small working pottery near St Nicholas Abbey creating hand made glazed items using the local red clay. Candle holders, lamp shades, vases and pots are among the items produced. Open: Daily, 10am–4.30pm.

Daphne's Sea Shell Studio (Congo Road, St Philip) Started by Daphne Hunte in 1980 and now with her daughters, this family business produces a range of decorative goods and jewellery using shells and fish scales. Daphne's shell "floral" arrangement mounted in shadow boxes are well known by collectors and past customers include Presidents of the United States. The studio also produces "petal porcelain" silk flower decorations. Open: Weekdays and Saturday morning.
Tel: 423-6180.

Earthworks Pottery (Edgehill, St Thomas) This small studio pottery sits on a hillside with superb distant views towards Bridgetown. Run by Goldie Spieler and her son, David, the pottery uses red clays to produce a wide range of low-fired earthenware from functional tableware to decorative pieces. The former items are domestic dishwasher safe and oven/microwave proof. Continued

Earthworks Pottery (continued)   Beside the working studio stands the "Potter's House Gallery" which is a small shop also selling refreshments. Sit on the gallery with a light snack and enjoy the views. Open: Weekdays and Saturday morning. Tel: 425-0223.

Fairfield Pottery & Gallery (Fairfield Cross Roads, St Michael)   This pottery is run by the Bell family – Denis and Sheila Bell with two of their children, Maggie and Peter. In addition to a range of decorative pottery goods, they produce huge and magnificent urns. They use local clay which they process themselves. Open: Monday to Friday, about 8.30am to 4pm. Tel: 424-3800.

Medford Mahogany Craft Village (Barbarees Hill, St Michael)   This is a rare opportunity to see wood carvers skilfully producing figurines, clocks and other items from mahogany tree roots that weigh some 3-4 tons. The mahogany tree was introduced to the island around 1790 but is now common, growing to a height of 60-70ft (20m). Open: Weekdays and Saturday morning. Tel: 427-1379.

Pelican Village (Princess Alice Highway, Bridgetown)   This is a cluster of over 30 small studios/shops, many of which are owner run – located on the road that leads from the Deep Water Harbour to the city centre. Locally made goods on sale include paintings, clothing, jewellery, leather and wooden products, hand-painted shirts, shell ornaments, figurines, batik and much more. Open: normal shopping hours.

The Potters at Chalky Mount (St Andrew)   Potters have been working here since the last century producing utilitarian and decorative work from the local red clay. This clay is found only in this part of the otherwise coralstone island. Open: Most days.

Pride Craft shops   The Government's Handicrafts Division run a number of shops under the *Pride Craft* name, stocking the craft work of local artists. Shop locations include the Airport, Harrison's Cave, Heywoods and in Bridgetown itself.

The Shell Gallery (Carlton House, Near Lower Carlton, St James)   Run by a keen shell collector, Maureen Edghill, the gallery features both local shells and those from other

parts of the world. In addition to made-up shell items such as her shell mirrors, she also sells individual shells. This nicely laid out gallery is well worth a visit if you are keen on sea shells. Open: Monday to Friday, 9am-4pm. Tel: 422-2635.

Wild Feathers (Long Bay, St Philip)   Near Sam Lord's Castle, the Skeete family produces wood carvings and paintings of indigenous and migratory birds.   The bird carvings are meticulous and lifelike. Other "bird art" items are on sale too. Open: Monday to Saturday, 9.30am–4.30pm. Tel: 423-7758.

Wood Dove carving by Wild Feathers.

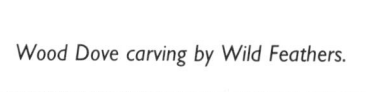

ATLANTIS SUBMARINE

Note the large viewing portholes.

Seating 28 people in its spacious air-conditioned cabin, the Atlantis II submarine dives a dozen times daily down to the reef off the west coast of the island. The Atlantis was constructed in Canada at a cost of approximately US$3 million. It is one of an increasing fleet of similar vessels operating around the world. The first in the series, Atlantis I, started services in the Cayman Islands in 1985 and Atlantis II made her first dive off Barbados in December 1986.

For the new submariner, the journey commences at the Atlantis offices (Horizon House on McGregor Street) in Bridgetown, from where passengers are taken on an enjoyable 15 minute trip by motor launch to where the Atlantis is waiting off the west coast. Once all are on board, the submarine dives gently down to the reef, some 130 feet (40m) below.

Through the sixteen 2ft (0.6m) diameter portholes passengers see the reef life, coral formations, shoals of fish and a sunken wreck. Cruising at only 1½ knots, the 49 ton submarine gives you plenty of time to look around. For the non-scuba diver, this is a unique opportunity to see these underwater sights at close quarters. Night time dives give a new perspective.

For many people this will be their first submarine trip so to celebrate this the Atlantis presents each new submariner with a dive certificate.

Dives: *Approximately 10-12 times daily (including some week-ends).*
Time to allow: *1 hour dive plus trip to & from sub = 1¾-2 hours.*
Facilities: *Souvenir shop on shore. Toilets on shore (none on sub). No refreshments.*
Note: *Children under 4 years or less than 3ft (90cm) in height not permitted.*
Cost: *Phone for details as special prices for Seniors, honeymooners, children etc.*
Telephone: *For information: 436-8932   For Reservations: 436-8929*

BAJAN HELICOPTER TOURS

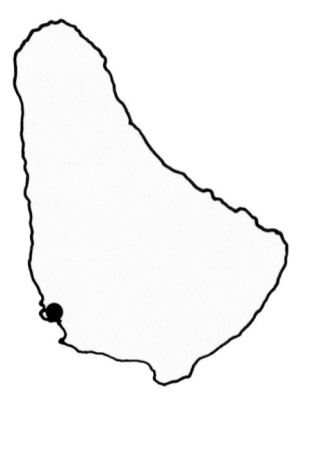

Another group of sightseers board a helicopter.

This is an interesting and novel way to see the sights if your time on the island is short. If your stay is longer, it's a great way to get your bearings and help you decide which attractions you want to visit when you are back on *terra firma*. Or you might wish to take the tour just for the sheer fun of it as you will see sights which are not possible from ground level.

Operating from their heliport at the Wharf, the company provides aerial tours of the island in their 5/6-seater jet helicopters. Bajan Helicopters offer two alternative tours – the "half island tour" which lasts about 20 minutes and the "full island tour" which takes 30 minutes. During the flight passengers hear an in-depth commentary through headsets.

On the shorter tour the helicopter flies over the centre of the island, across the hilly Scotland district towards the east coast then west across to Speightstown. From there it turns south flying back to Bridgetown via the west coast and finally over the cruise ships in the port. The longer 30 minute tour first heads along the south coast towards Sam Lord's Castle then northwards via Bathsheba up the east coast. From there it follows the same route as the shorter "half island tour" back to Bridgetown.

With these tours it is recommended that you book a day in advance to be sure you fly at the time you wish.

Flights: *Monday to Saturday, 9am–5pm.*
Time to allow: *About 30-45 minutes minimum, but waiting time may extend this.*
Facilities: *Small gift shop. Toilets. Refreshments.*
Entrance Fee: *20 minute flight Bds$130.   30 minute flight Bds$200.*
Telephone: *431-0069*

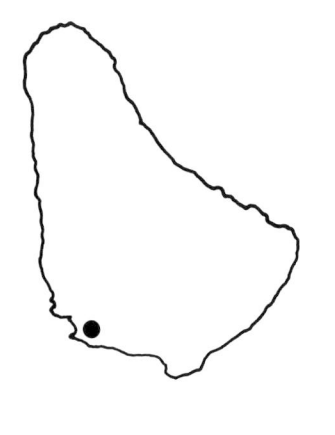

The impressive Museum building was originally part of St Ann's Garrison.

Appropriately the Museum is housed in a building which itself is of historical interest. British troops were stationed in Barbados intermittently from 1651 to 1905. The museum buildings were built as a military prison between 1817 and 1853 as part of the St Ann's Garrison and became the Barbados Museum in 1933. One of the prison cells has been preserved.

The Museum has an excellent natural history display describing the coral structure of Barbados and life on land and sea around the island. There are also interesting artifacts from the early Amerindian inhabitants and memorabilia representing all stages of the island's social, economic and political history. There is a military history gallery, an African gallery and collections of china, glass and decorative arts. Several rooms depict the furnishings of a Plantation House, there is a gallery specifically for children and another gallery for temporary exhibitions. It is all well laid out and described.

Of particular interest is the Museum's collection of rare historical maps of the island and the Reference Library which is available for research on the island's history or genealogy.

Although not air-conditioned, the Museum is well cooled by fans and the natural airflow.

On two evenings each week the Museum courtyard becomes the stage setting for the dinner show "1627 and all that" (see the chapter EVENING ENTERTAINMENT).

Open: *Monday to Saturday, 10am–6pm.*
Time to allow: *1½-2 hours minimum.*
Facilities: *Gift shop. Toilets. Refreshments.*
Note: *Ramps allow access for baby pushchairs and wheelchairs.*
Entrance Fee: *Bds$7. Children Bds$1.*
Telephone: *427-0201 or 436-1956*

BARBADOS WILDLIFE RESERVE

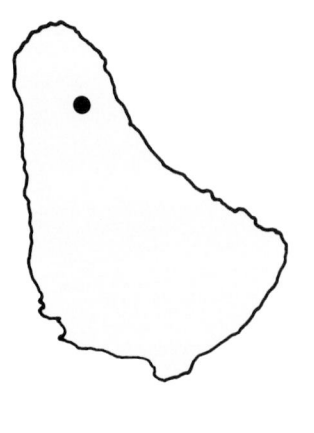

A Green Monkey watches school children and visitors nearby.

This is neither a zoo nor a safari park but a dense four acre mahogany wood where a surprising number of animals roam freely. Visitors can observe these animals at very close quarters from the many paths that traverse the Reserve. It is the creation of Canadian primatologist Jean Baulu and his wife Suzanne.

The animals, birds and reptiles represent species to be found in Barbados, the wider Caribbean and other parts of the world. Some creatures such as the Brown Pelican and Raccoon were once common in Barbados but are now only to be seen in the Reserve. This is also home for some 50 Green Monkeys. It is thought that there are around 8,000 of these monkeys on the island but they are classed as pests due to the damage they cause to crops.

In or near the ponds are otters and caymans (like alligators). Some of the tortoises were donated to the Reserve by the author's wife, Charlotte, who reared them from eggs. A few of the animals and birds are caged. In the walk-in aviary can be seen lots of tropical birds including toucans, macaws, cockatoos and Amazon parrots.

The walk around the Reserve is mainly outside but is very shaded, making this a cool excursion even during the middle of the day.

Please note: The animals are not tame and visitors should heed the warning notices in the Reserve.

The Grenade Hall Forest and Signal Station are immediately adjacent to the Wildlife Reserve – see the separate entry later in this chapter.

Open: *Daily (including week-ends), 10am–5pm.*
Time to allow: *1-2 hours minimum.*
Facilities: *Small gift shop. Toilets. Refreshments.*
Note: *Path is difficult for baby pushchairs or wheelchairs.*
Entrance Fee: *Bds$10. Children half price.*
Telephone: *422-8826*

BARBADOS ZOO PARK & OUGHTERSON

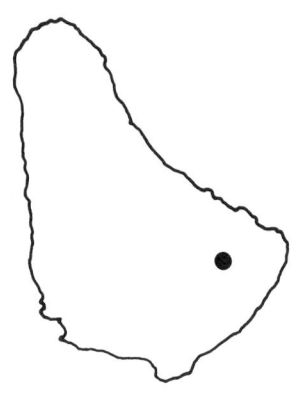

Two zebras graze with Oughterson Plantation House behind.

This is two attractions in one! – A small informal zoo and a plantation house situated in a breezy country location. Oughterson was a sugar plantation before the well-known American naturalist, Bill Miller, created the Zoo Park. The present owners are Michael and Ann Shemilt.

Although small, the zoo has a wide variety of animals ranging from local animals such as the mongoose, Blackbelly sheep (a breed only found in Barbados) and the green monkey to zebras from Africa. There are also parrots, snakes, crocodiles and the amazing Brazilian tapirs . . . . to mention just a few.

The zoo is set in the grounds of the original plantation house and part is a nature trail through fruit trees where peacocks, ducks and guineafowl roam.

The plantation house itself is unusual. It comprises an early 18th century two-storey block with a 19th century single storey addition to the front. It was thought that this addition would make the house more resistant to hurricanes in its exposed site. Only the ground floor is open to the public as the house is lived in. Some of the furniture is contemporary with the house. The huge open fireplace in the former kitchen is of particular interest.

Open: *Daily (including week-ends), 9.30am–5pm.*
Time to allow: *1-1 ½ hours.*
Facilities: *Toilets. Refreshments. No shop.*
Note: *The nature trail is difficult for baby pushchairs and wheelchairs.*
Entrance Fee: *Bds$8. Children (under 12) half price, (under 2) free.*
Telephone: *423-6203*

BRIDGETOWN CENTRE (see also chapter SHOPPING)

Bridgetown is the capital of Barbados. The name was reputedly chosen because the first settlers found a bridge, built by the early Amerindian inhabitants, spanning the waterway. Right from the beginning, 100 acres on the north side of the river were reserved for a settlement and within only a few decades the population was over 2,000 and there were stores, taverns and churches. The rapid growth continued despite several devastating fires and hurricanes. Notably the fire of 1668 that destroyed 80% of the then 1,000 buildings after igniting the gunpowder in the Public Magazine. Another major fire in 1766 ruined 26 acres of the city centre in one night. There were other lesser fires, but the major fire of 1860 provided government with the opportunity to purchase land by the Careenage for the erection of the Parliament Buildings.

The town officially became the City of Bridgetown in 1842 by royal decree. Today, Bridgetown is a busy bustling city with much for the visitor to see in the centre in addition to the shops and restaurants. . . .

Careenage   At the centre of the city is the Careenage *(right)*, which was the island's main harbour until the construction of the Deep Water Harbour (from 1956 to '61). Inter-island schooners berthed here until very recently. The name is derived from the word "careen" that means to turn a boat on its side to scrape her hull and repaint her. Today it is home for a number of fishing boats, the Coast Guard's vessels and numerous private yachts. Here there

are yachts and fishing boats for charter (refer to the chapter SPORTS & ACTIVITIES).

Central Bank Building & Frank Collymore Hall   Completed in 1986, this is the tallest building on the island and towers over the capital. Besides many offices it also houses the Frank Collymore Hall, which is a 500-seat Concert Hall named after the renowned Barbadian poet, actor and teacher. For information about the excellent and exciting performances to see, refer to the newspapers.

Chamberlain Bridge & Independence Arch   The bridge was opened in 1872 as a Swing Bridge and renamed in 1900 after the British Secretary of State for the Colonies who had helped the island's economy at that time. The bridge no longer swings open. The decorated arch over the approach road to the Chamberlain Bridge was constructed in 1987 to commemorate the island's 21st anniversary of independence.

Nelson's Statue   *(Left)* Like Nelson's Column in London, this statue stands in Trafalgar Square, but it was unveiled in 1813 and therefore predates the one in London. Although Nelson had little connection with Barbados, grateful islanders erected the statue as they felt the timely appearance of his fleet in 1805 had deterred a possible French invasion of Barbados. Interestingly the bronze statue (by Richard Westmacott) shows the famous British admiral with two good eyes but without his right arm, though he was in fact blinded *before* losing the arm!

The National Flag of Barbados   The ultramarine outer panels represent the sea and sky of Barbados, while the gold centre panel is for the sand of its beaches. Neptune's Trident appeared in the Seal when the island was a colony. The broken shaft indicates a break with the past.

The Barbados Coat of Arms   The Golden Shield of the Arms carries two Pride of Barbados flowers (the National Flower) and the Bearded Fig Tree (which was common at the time of the island's settlement). On either side of the shield is a Dolphin (to symbolise the fishing industry – this is a local fish, not the porpoise-like mammal) and a Pelican (there used to be Pelican Island, now incorporated in the Deep Water Harbour). Above the shield and helmet is an arm holding two pieces of sugar-cane. The sugar-cane is held in the shape of St Andrew's Cross as Independence Day is celebrated on St Andrew's Day, 30th November.

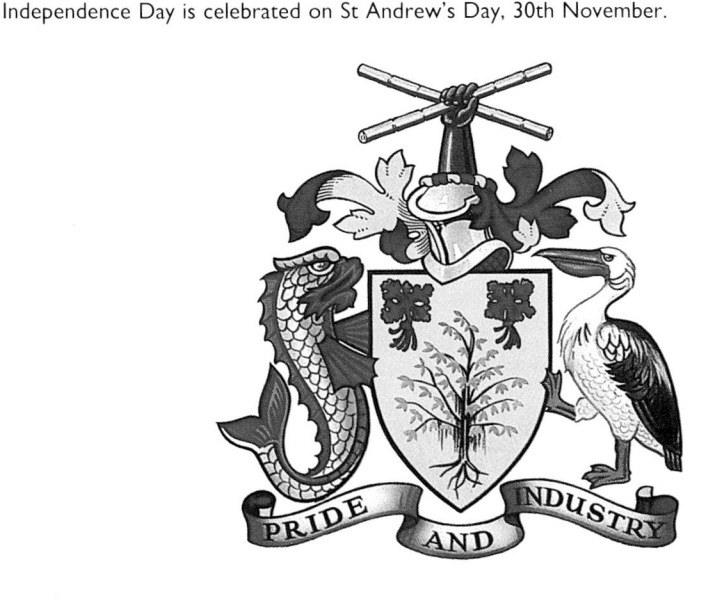

BRIDGETOWN CENTRE (continued)

Parliament Buildings   Barbados has the third oldest parliament in the Commonwealth, after Britain and Bermuda. It was founded in 1639. The present buildings were finished in 1871 (the West Building) and 1874 (the East Building). The buildings are not open to the public when Parliament is sitting.

Most of the main government ministries and the Prime Minister's Office are located in Government Headquarters on Bay Street. The official residence of the Prime Minister is Ilaro Court, located at Two Mile Hill. Government House, by Government Hill, has been the Governor's, and later the Governor-General's, residence since 1703.

Queen's Park   *(Left)* The house in Queen's Park was originally the headquarters and residence of the British General who commanded the garrison. After the withdrawal of British troops in 1905, it was purchased by Government and the grounds were opened as a public park in 1909. Today the main building houses a theatre and gallery. The grounds also contain the "Steel Shed" which is another theatre and a massive Baobab tree with a girth of over 60ft (18m).

St Mary's Church   Although this church was only built in 1825, it is on the site of the first church of Bridgetown, called St Michael's Church. This first church was built around 1630 but was abandoned later that century when the new church (see below) was built on a different site. The original graveyard continued to be used for the town's coloured population.

St Michael's Cathedral   This Anglican Cathedral is the second church to be built on this site. The first was consecrated in 1665 but was destroyed in the great hurricane of 1780. Prior to being demolished by natural causes the building was almost destroyed in the 1750s due to incompetent major repair work, its huge roof span being the main problem. The new building was erected shortly after the 1780 hurricane but was also dogged by structural problems. It has been a Cathedral since 1825.

St Patrick's Cathedral   The original Roman Catholic church was opened on St Patrick's Day in 1848 and consecrated two years later, but was destroyed by fire in 1897. The present building was completed in 1899 and became a Cathedral in 1970.

Screw Dock   This dry dock worked by screw action. It was built between 1889 and 1893 and at the time of its ceasing work in the 1980s was thought to be unique in the world. It could lift almost 1,000 tons.

The Synagogue   The original synagogue on this site dated from the 1650s and was one of the first two in the Western Hemisphere (the other being in Curaçao). It was destroyed in the great hurricane of 1831. The present building, erected on the old foundations, was opened in 1833. In 1929, as there was only one practising Jew left on the island, the building was sold and converted into offices. Continued . . .

The Synagogue (continued)

By the early 1980s the building was derelict but was restored by the local Jewish community with the support of the Barbados National Trust, the Caribbean Conservation Commission and Government. The building is now back in use again as a synagogue. It is open to the public, from Monday to Friday, 9am-4pm.

(The photo shows the Synagogue with the Jewish Cemetery in the foreground).

Trafalgar Square   Near to Nelson's Statue is the Fountain Garden installed in the square in 1865 to commemorate the introduction of piped water to the capital in 1861. In Trafalgar Square is also to be found the Cenotaph war memorial.

View across the Careenage   This view *(below)* shows the Parliament Buildings (West and East). The East Building when it was completed in 1874 had a large clock tower but it began to subside and was taken down in 1884. One of the two towers on the West Building, which had originally looked similar to each other, was then modified to accommodate the clock, where it remains to this day. The Central Bank Building is clearly visible on the right. This new building towers over the city. Nelson's Statue and the Cenotaph are also visible.

CODRINGTON COLLEGE & GROUNDS

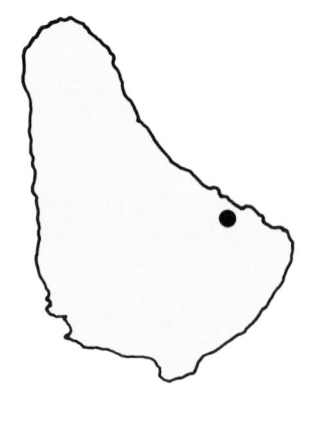

The impressive avenue of palms leading down to the College.

If driving on the eastern side of St John, a diversion to see this historic College and wander through its grounds will make a pleasant interlude. Codrington is the theological college of the Anglican Church in the Province of the West Indies.

Access to the buildings is very limited due to their use by the students. A visit to Codrington is therefore primarily to look at the general layout and to stroll through the grounds, spot the many large fish in the lily pond and enjoy the fine view over Conset Bay. A Nature Trail takes one through 5 acres of woodland that contain many interesting trees, including a massive Silk Cotton tree.

Christopher Codrington was a Barbadian planter who became Governor-General of the Leeward Islands. He was born in 1668 and lived as a child in the original mansion house that is now the College Principal's Lodge. When Codrington died (in the same house in 1710) he bequeathed his plantations to an Anglican missionary body and charged it with, among other things, setting up a College of Divinity.

The main buildings, situated at the end of an impressive avenue of palm trees, were inspired by an Oxford quadrangle though funding allowed only one side of the proposed quad to be built (between 1714 and 1743). The College opened on a modest scale in 1745 but not until 1830 did it become an institution of higher education. From 1875 to 1955 the College was affiliated to the University of Durham in England. Since 1955 it has concentrated on theology and is now affiliated to the University of the West Indies. It has recently undergone a $1 million restoration.

Open: *Daily (including week-ends), 10am–4pm.*
Time to allow: *½-1 hour minimum.*
Facilities: *Toilets. No refreshments. No shop.*
Entrance Fee: *Bds$5. Children (under 16) free.*
Telephone: *433-1274*

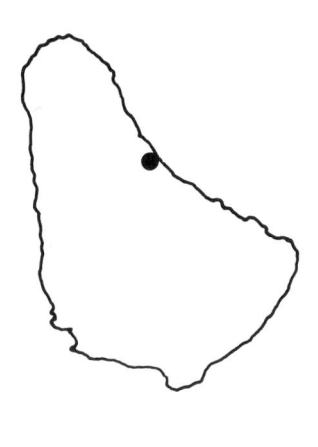

The East Coast seen from south of Bathsheba.

A drive along the East Coast Road should be a "must" for every visitor as it shows completely different aspects of the island – the surf of the Atlantic Ocean breaking on miles of deserted beaches, the exhilarating sea breeze and the rugged landscape. There is a great feeling of spaciousness.

It's a pleasant, relaxing place to visit, an excellent spot to picnic and you can dip in one of the many rock pools (but see the Caution below).

The East Coast road was opened by HM Queen Elizabeth II and follows the line of the one-track railway *(seen in the old photo below)* that once ran from Bridgetown to Belleplaine in St Andrew. The railway was opened in the 1880s carrying both sugar and passengers but was closed in 1937 due to the ever increasing use of road transport. Today little of it remains but an important legacy was the development of Bathsheba as a seaside resort for Barbadians with many "bay houses" being built there and some hotels being opened, such as the Atlantis.

Heading north from Bathsheba one passes through an area called Cattlewash with several "bay houses". Beyond is Barclays Park, a 50 acre public picnic site, donated by Barclays Bank on the occasion of the island's independence. The park is a busy place at week-ends and on public holidays. Here there are toilets and a "snackette" which is open every day. North of the park is the distinctive hillside shoulder of Chalky Mount and the sandy expanse of Walker's Savannah. The road then curves inland towards Belleplaine.

Caution: *There are very dangerous currents on this coast so sea bathing should be restricted to paddling or dips in rock pools when the tide is coming in. Swimming is very dangerous.*

FARLEY HILL PARK

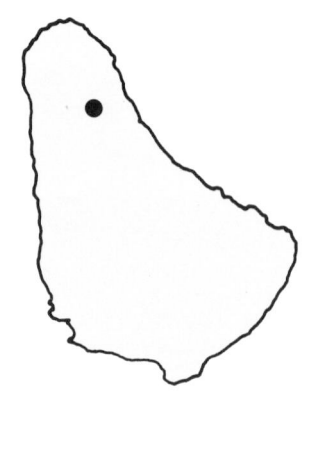

The once great house of Farley Hill, now a dramatic ruin.

This is a pleasant and cool park where you can relax and picnic in shady wooded areas with benches. From the path on the eastern side there are spectacular views of the Scotland district, the East Coast and the Atlantic giving a great feeling of being on top of the island. The ruins of Farley Hill house add to the interest.

The earliest part of this once great house was built about 1818, with many new rooms and the south wing being added during the next 40-50 years. By the mid nineteenth century Farley Hill was regarded as the most imposing mansion on the island and the owner, Sir Graham Briggs, entertained many people including royalty. Sir Graham not only improved the house but also developed the gardens, importing many new trees and plants to the island, such as the traveller's palm, sago and date palms and Norfolk Island pine. The indigenous Farleyense fern was discovered here.

The house was lived in until the 1930s but thereafter only intermittently. During the last war many of the fine trees were cut down for firewood and the house became dilapidated. In 1956 it was partly restored for some of the sequences in the film "Island in the Sun", but it was subsequently destroyed by fire.

In 1965 the Government of Barbados purchased the property and declared it a national park and it was officially opened by HM Queen Elizabeth II the following year.

Farley Hill is easy to drive to and conveniently sited opposite the Barbados Wildlife Reserve & Grenade Hall.

Open: *Daily (including week-ends).*
Facilities: *Toilets. No refreshments. No shop.*
Entrance Fee: *Cars Bds$3 per day.*
Telephone: *422-3555*

FLOWER FOREST

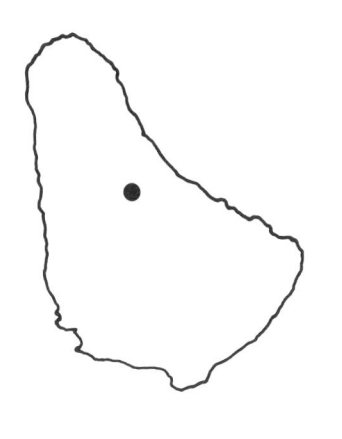

Visitors on one of the well-maintained paths in the Forest.

Far away from the beaches and the bustle of Bridgetown is a quiet oasis where you can spend some time walking, looking at plants and enjoying the views. The aptly named Flower Forest is located on a hillside in the picturesque Scotland district. Temperatures are a little cooler than at sea-level due to the elevation (850 ft, 260m) and there is plenty of shade along the various walks.

The Flower Forest was opened in 1983 on the site of Richmond Plantation, after two years of preparation. It is a 50 acre site of which nearly half is already landscaped. Paths wind through the forest between masses of flowering plants, bananas, guavas, citrus and many other tropical trees. All plants are labelled and there is a free guide sheet on specific plants to look out for so you can wander at your own pace.

From this tranquil setting you get fine views of the area, including a sight of Mount Hillaby, which at 1,116ft (340m) is the highest point on the island. At the northern end of the forest there is a panoramic viewpoint with the Atlantic Ocean in the distance.

There are seats and benches throughout the forest. As a nice extra touch, umbrellas and walking sticks can be borrowed from the ticket desk. After your walk through the forest you can have a snack and cooling drink and admire the view from the terrace of the Administration building.

Open: *Daily (including week-ends), 9am–5pm.*
Time to allow: *1-2 hours.*
Facilities: *Best of Barbados gift shop. Toilets (for disabled too). Refreshments.*
Note: *Paths now suitable for baby pushchairs and wheelchairs.*
Entrance Fee: *Bds$10. Children (under 16) half price.*
Telephone: *433-8152*

FRANCIA PLANTATION HOUSE

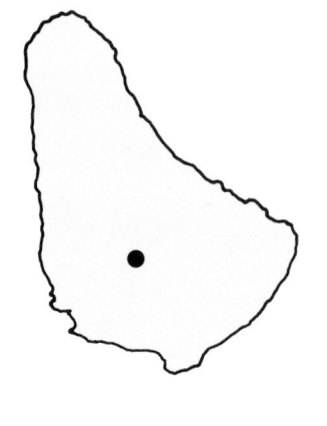

Francia was one of the last plantation great houses to be built in Barbados.

This is an attractive and interesting plantation house, lived in by descendants of the original owner. "Francia" is derived from the Portuguese word "frança" meaning France, as the original owner was a Frenchman who became a successful rancher in Brazil before he met and married a Barbadian.

This international background shows in the architectural features of the house, for instance the double "Demerara" shutters (so called as these were the style of shutter developed in Demerara county, Guyana) and the extensive use of South American woods on the walls and ceiling of the entrance hall. Francia is a relatively recent plantation house, having been built in the early part of this century.

As the house is lived in, only the ground floor and gardens are open to the public for the guided tour. The dining room and drawing room are furnished with fine antiques. Of particular interest is the collection of antique maps that are on display. Outside the house there is a set of original drip-stones that was once the standard way to provide cool and filtered drinking water.

The house is beautifully maintained and sits in spacious elegant gardens with lawns, terraces and fountains. An added bonus is the panoramic view over the St George valley.

Francia is still a working plantation, though today vegetables rather than sugarcane are grown.

Open: *Monday to Friday, 10am–4pm.*
Time to allow: *½-1 hour.*
Facilities: *Toilets. No shop. No refreshments, but nearby is Tony-Anne's Restaurant and bar.*
Entrance Fee: *Bds$6. Children half price.*
Telephone: *429-0474*

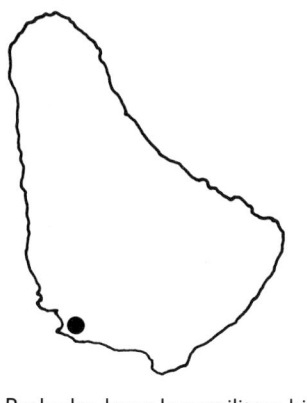

The Main Guard, part of the National Cannon Collection and the edge of the race course.

Barbados has a long military history and many buildings and fortifications remain, although since the departure of British troops in 1905-06 some of the buildings have been put to more peaceful uses. The fortifications at Charles Fort, at the southern end of Carlisle Bay, date from 1650. About ½ mile (0.8km) inland is the main Garrison site which was acquired in the late 1700s as a result of France declaring war on Britain in 1778. Construction then began of the many barracks, stores and residences, with more land being purchased in the early 1800s. Ultimately it was a huge walled area stretching from Charles Fort (by today's Hilton Hotel) to encompass a sizeable area around the Savannah.

Sometimes 2,500 or more men were garrisoned here, often just under canvas. The ravages of disease and occasional hurricanes claimed thousands of lives during the 19th century. In times of epidemics some of the troops were evacuated to Gun Hill, near to the Signal Station.

Today the Garrison is being restored and preserved and there are plans for a visitor centre at the Main Guard and in addition a Military Museum to be housed in the old magazine of St Ann's Fort. The Barbados Museum is already housed in what was the military prison. Part of the Garrison area is not normally accessible to the public as it is the base of the Barbados Defence Force, but there is still a lot that can be seen.

The Savannah   Originally this was used as a parade ground and for accommodating troops under canvas. It is now the island's race course and hosts kite-flying at Easter, rugby matches and many other public events, including the annual Independence parades.

National Cannon Collection   Over 30 cannon have been mounted at the western edge of the Savannah. The Collection is the largest in existence of 17th century English iron guns; it includes a cannon with Cromwell's Republican Arms on it, one of only two known to be still extant.

For a detailed guide refer to the excellent illustrated booklet by Warren Alleyne and Jill Sheppard titled "The Barbados Garrison and its Buildings", available from the Barbados Museum shop.

Main Guard & Military Museum
Opening hours: Not open as yet.
For information: Contact the Garrison Secretary on 426-0982.

GRENADE HALL FOREST & SIGNAL STATION

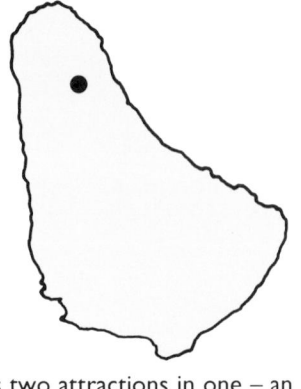

The Signal Station stands on high ground with commanding views.

Located adjacent to the Barbados Wildlife Reserve, this is two attractions in one – an early 19th century signal station and an educational nature trail. The signal station was restored in 1992 by the Wildlife Reserve with the co-operation of the Barbados National Trust. Built in 1819, Grenade Hall was one of the six signal stations on the island. It was of similar design to the Cotton Tower but different to Gun Hill (see opposite).

The building of the chain of signal stations from Speightstown in the north to St Ann's Fort in the south was triggered by the slave rebellion of 1816 which, although it was unsuccessful, gave the authorities a shock. The signal stations had other important signalling duties – warning military headquarters of an enemy fleet, informing Bridgetown businesses of the impending arrival of merchant ships, telling people the time by hoisting "time balls" and to summon members of the Governor's Council to meetings.

There was accommodation for two signalmen. Slits in the walls pointed to neighbouring signal stations and signalling was by flags, though it seems that semaphore arms on the mast were also used. At night they probably used lights. As with Gun Hill, the signal station became obsolete when the telephone was introduced to the island.

The Grenade Hall Forest covers several acres through which there is a 1¼ mile (2km) paved trail. Here the mysteries of the plant world and ecosystem are explained by signs which describe the delicate balance of nature. Dozens of species of trees, shrubs, vines and herbs can be seen as well as Amerindian caves. The whole intention of the Grenade Hall Forest is to increase environmental awareness but to do it in a fun way.

Open: *Daily (including week-ends), 10am–5pm.*
Time to allow: *1-2 hours minimum.*
Facilities: *Small gift shop. Toilets. Refreshments.*
Note: *Path is difficult for baby pushchairs or wheelchairs.*
Entrance Fee: *Bds$10. Children half price.*
Telephone: *422-8826*

GUN HILL SIGNAL STATION

The approach to the Signal Station at Gun Hill.

This Signal Station was restored from a ruin by the Barbados National Trust in 1983. Gun Hill is not only an interesting piece of military history but from its strategic hilltop position it also commands magnificent views over the whole of the southern part of the island. Schomburgk, the noted historian, commented in the mid 19th century that "no stranger who visits Barbados should omit to see this spot".

Built in 1818, Gun Hill was one of six signal stations though today only it, the Cotton Tower (also a National Trust property) and Grenade Hall (see opposite) have been preserved.

For a general description of signal stations see the Grenade Hall entry opposite. Gun Hill was also used as a convalescent site for British troops who were normally garrisoned down at the Savannah and subject to occasional ravages of yellow fever.

By 1854, as an economy measure, the military had given up their interest in the signal stations. Even their use for civil duties (such as hurricane warning) effectively disappeared with the advent of the telephone service in Barbados in 1883.

The Lion Below the Signal Station is the famous lion, carved from sold coralstone in 1868 by a Captain Henry Wilkinson aided by four military labourers. There is a Latin inscription on the base which gives Wilkinson's name and a biblical reference which appears to allude to Britain's imperial domination of the world at that time.

Open: *Monday to Friday, 9am–5pm.*
Time to allow: *½-1 hour (mainly outside walk).*
Facilities: *Toilets. No shop. No refreshments, but on the road to Francia is Tony-Anne's Restaurant and bar.*
Entrance Fee: *Bds$5. Child (under 12) ½ price, (under 6) free.*
Telephone: *429-1358 (Trust HQ: 426-2421 or 436-9033)*

HARRISON'S CAVE

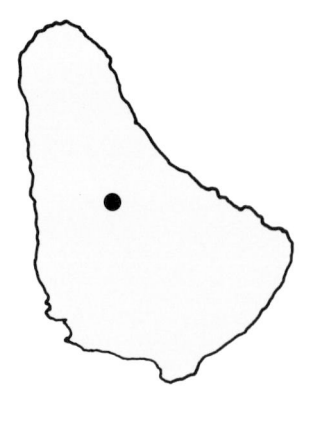

Special lighting makes the most of the cave's scenery.

An underground tram tour through this extraordinary natural cave is both exciting and memorable. Although originally discovered nearly 200 years ago, the cave was largely forgotten until rediscovered by a Dane, Ole Sorensen, in 1970. With the initial stimulus of the Barbados National Trust the development of the cave by Government began in the mid '70s and it was opened to the public in 1981.

Today the cave is administered by the National Conservation Commission who run an open-top electric tram through the well-lit half mile series of wide tunnels and chambers. A guide provides a commentary and the tram stops at several points for visitors to get out and savour the spectacular surroundings.

There are large and impressive crystal stalactites, stalagmites, rushing streams, waterfalls, placid turquoise pools and huge vaulted chambers, about 250 foot long by 100 foot high (75 x 30m). Cleverly concealed lighting enhances the whole effect.

Caves, such as Harrison's, form over millions of years due to the action of rain-water seeping into the limestone (coral) cap of the island which is some 300ft (90m) thick. The rain-water becomes mildly acidic having absorbed carbon dioxide and this erodes the limestone forming ever larger chambers as the rain-water flows into underground streams.

Harrison's Cave is quite cool and droplets of clean water may fall, but your usual clothes should be quite sufficient for comfort. Hard hats are provided as a safety precaution.

It is advisable to phone in advance to book on a tour as this is one of the island's most popular attractions.

Open: *Daily (including week-ends), from 9am. Last tour 4pm.*
Time to allow: *Tour about 1 hour, but allow for delays prior to tour starting.*
Facilities: *Craft shop. Toilets. Refreshments.*
Entrance Fee: *Bds$15. Children (under 16) half price.*
Telephone: *438-6640/1/2/3/4/5*

HOLETOWN & ST JAMES CHURCH

St James Church at Holetown. A lovely coralstone building.

Holetown, in the parish of St James, is historically important as the site where the first English landed and claimed the island for the King and also where the first settlers chose to land in 1627. Originally called Jamestown after King James I, it later became The Hole and then Holetown.

Part of the present day Holetown Police Station was James Fort, one of a string of fortifications built in the 17th and 18th centuries on the west and south coasts of the island. Near the Police Station is a monument erected in 1905 which was then thought to be the 300th anniversary of the initial landing. It was later learned that the first landing was more likely to have been twenty years later, in 1625.

At Sunset Crest are two large shopping complexes that can supply most visitors' needs with a big supermarket (Super Centre), a branch of Cave Shepherd, bank, boutiques and pharmacy etc.

The Anglican Parish Church of St James is well worth a visit. It stands on one of the oldest pieces of consecrated land on the island at the site of the first settlement. The original wooden building was replaced by a stone Church in the late 17th century. This building was then destroyed in the great hurricane of 1780 but the Church was rebuilt and the building you see today has the same lower walls. The sanctuary and north porch were added later and the nave roof was raised on new pillars and arches in the late 19th century.

The Church has undergone considerable restoration during the 1980s – a credit to its rector and congregation. Of particular interest is the Baptismal Font dating from 1684 and the original church bell dated 1696, thereby predating the famous American "Liberty Bell".

President and Mrs Reagan worshipped here during their visit to Barbados.

JOLLY ROGER & BAJAN QUEEN CRUISES

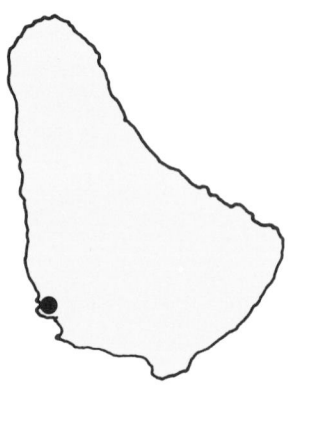

The Jolly Roger with a swash-buckling crew off the west coast.

A cruise on the pirate ship *Jolly Roger* is one of those things that almost every visitor to Barbados for over two decades has experienced and enjoyed. It's also a great favourite with many locals. With lots of free drink, loud music, energetic dancing and a "pirate" host, the party atmosphere makes a memorable trip.

The *Jolly Roger* sets off from the Shallow Draft Harbour on the north side of Bridgetown. As she clears the harbour and picks up the breeze the sails are hoisted and she cruises slowly up the west coast. The merry pirate ship anchors off Holetown where a barbecue buffet is served. There is the opportunity to "walk the plank", for rope swinging, snorkelling and a trip to the beach. The sun can be very hot but there is some covered cabin space and the sails also cast a little shade. The uninitiated should note that the tasty rum punch served free on board is stronger than it appears!

For something a little more elegant, the *Bajan Queen* is a replica Mississippi-style river boat that makes romantic evening dinner cruises up the west coast with dancing to a live band, DJ and free drinks.

The island looks very pretty from off shore, whether by day or night. Flying fish can sometimes be seen. Sunsets are often spectacular and if there is a moon the atmosphere is quite enchanting.

Sailing Times:
Jolly Roger: Sets sail daily at 10am (excluding Sunday),
         but vital to phone in advance.
Bajan Queen: Wednesday and Saturday evenings.

The Bajan Queen evening cruise.

Time to allow: About 4 hours.

Facilities: Toilets (the "heads"). Food & drink provided.

Fares: Bds$105. Child (7-14) Bds$55, (4-6) Bds$20, (to4) free.

Note: Both ships are available for day or evening charter.

Telephone: 436-6424

MORGAN LEWIS SUGAR WINDMILL

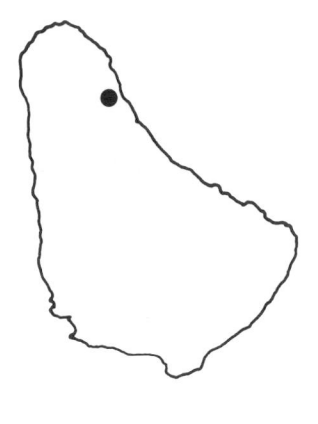

Morgan Lewis, the only completely preserved sugar windmill known to exist in the Caribbean.

This is a unique opportunity to see a preserved windmill with its sugar grinding machinery intact. The mill is perched on a breezy hillside overlooking the east coast and much of the parish of St Andrew. It was one of the last working mills in Barbados, stopping only in 1947 and was given to the Barbados National Trust by the late Mr E.L. Bannister. Morgan Lewis was one of the largest windmills.

At one time there were over 700 of these mills on the island. Their function was to grind the sugar cane prior to boiling. Now the process is carried out in the sugar factories but the coralstone walls of many mills can still be seen dotted around the countryside.

For safety reasons the canvas sails at Morgan Lewis have been removed, though the arms are still there. Inside the mill you can climb the staircase right up to the top and wonder at the sheer size and strength of the machinery. As you climb you get fine views down towards the east coast and the Atlantic Ocean.

There is also a collection of old photographs and a drawing of the mill's machinery. If you want to see what sugar mills were like in action, then visit nearby St Nicholas Abbey and view the 1934 film (shown twice daily) that includes sequences of working sugar mills.

Open: *Monday to Friday, 9am–4pm.*
Time to allow: *¼-½ hour.*
Facilities: *None.*
Entrance Fee: *Bds$2.*
Telephone: *National Trust HQ: 426-2421 or 436-9033*

NATIONAL TRUST OPEN HOUSES

Welches Plantation House, one of the popular houses opened to the public for one afternoon each year.

Each year, from January to April, the Barbados National Trust organises its "Open House Programme" enabling the public to visit some of the island's most interesting and beautiful private homes. It is a great opportunity to see around them and usually all the rooms and gardens are open to view.

The programme changes a little each year with different houses being opened, but is mainly a mixture of old plantation houses and more modern luxury homes. Some of the houses opened in recent years include: a) Heron Bay, built in 1947 by Ronald Tree, a former British MP and founder of the Barbados National Trust. It is an impressive and magnificent building set in 20 acres of parkland; b) Welches Plantation, which comprises an attractive plantation house, outbuildings and gardens. Welches is the home of artist Jill Walker and her husband Jimmy and is the administrative headquarters for their "Best of Barbados" shops. Other houses that have been opened in past years include: Porters – an old plantation house; Cockade House – an exquisite Palladian fantasy and Casuarina Heights – a modern luxury home with commanding views.

To find out which house is open on which date, contact the Barbados National Trust HQ for a copy of their Open House programme. This leaflet provides details of each of the properties to be opened and is also available from most hotel receptions.

The Trust organises a special bus tour for about Bds$35 which includes pick-ups from south and west coast hotels and the entrance fee to the Open House. All proceeds go to the Barbados National Trust.

Open: *Wednesdays, 2.30pm–5.30pm (January to April).*
Time to allow: *1 hour minimum.*
Facilities (vary): *Small shop and bookstall. Toilets. Light refreshments.*
Entrance Fee: *Bds$12 (includes a complimentary drink). Bds$4 for members of allied societies.*
Telephone: *National Trust HQ: 426-2421 or 436-9033*

PORTVALE SUGAR FACTORY
& SIR FRANK HUTSON SUGAR MACHINERY MUSEUM

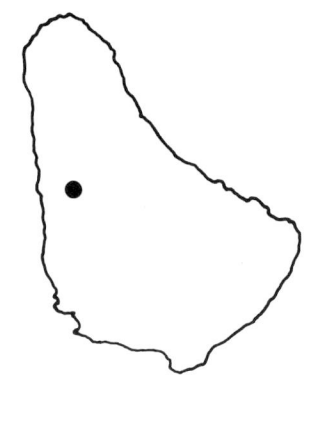

The factory can grind 150 tons of sugar-cane per hour.

The history of Barbados is synonymous with sugar and to see this important commodity being produced is an awe inspiring and memorable experience. There are now only three working sugar factories on the island of which the Portvale factory is the largest and most recent. Although it dates from 1983/84, it took its machinery from other factories and its name is a combination of two of those factories – Porters and Vaucluse.

The factory takes the raw sugar-cane and by a process of grinding the canes then boiling the resulting juice produces soft brown sugar and molasses (the latter being used to make rum). It takes 8½ to 9 tons of sugar-cane to make one ton of sugar. The mill extracts 98% of the sucrose of the cane and the residue (called "bagasse") is used as fuel to fire the steam boiler and generate electricity to power the factory. The factory is therefore self-sufficient from an energy standpoint.

In the 17th century the island produced about 10,000 tons of sugar per year and it took 20 tons of cane to make one ton of sugar. Production rose to some 75,000 tons by the following century. The 20th century saw production peaking at 200,000 tons (in 1957) but by 1993 this had dropped back to 49,000 tons – the worst crop this century.

Near the factory is the sugar machinery museum, which is a Barbados National Trust property. The machinery was gathered together by Sir Frank Hutson, a distinguished engineer. There is also an 8-minute video showing sugar being made.

Open: *Out-of-Crop time (about June to January), Monday to Friday, 9am–5pm.*
In-Crop time (about February to May), Daily (including week-ends), 9am–5pm.
Time to allow: *1-2 hours minimum.*
Facilities: *Small gift shop. Toilets. Light refreshments.*
Note: *Hard hats are provided. Closed shoes mandatory (ie no sandals).*
Entrance Fee: *Museum Bds$4. Factory Bds$4.*
Telephone: *National Trust HQ: 426-2421*

Sugar Cane

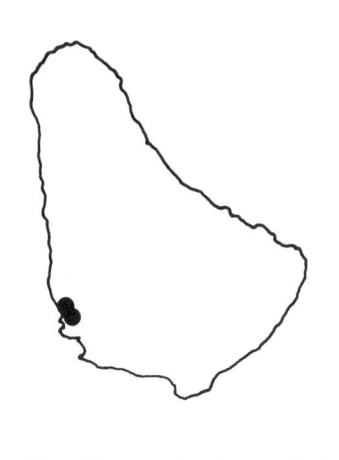

Entrance to the Mount Gay Rum Visitor Centre.

No visit to Barbados would be quite complete without a rum tour, due to the drink's historical importance to the island. The production of rum requires a ready supply of pure water and molasses. Both are readily available; the coral structure of Barbados has always ensured that its water is pure and the sugar industry has provided the black treacle-like molasses since the mid 17th century. It is therefore not surprising that rum has long been distilled in Barbados.

Today there are two distilleries on the island. The oldest, Mount Gay, dates back to 1663 and is probably the oldest rum distillery in the world. The Mount Gay tour starts in their "rumshop" theatre with an excellent short audio-visual presentation. This is a historical account, explaining the significant role that sugar and rum played in the development of the island. Visitors are then taken on a tour of the Ageing and Blending facility of Mount Gay to uncover the mysteries of rum making.

After fermentation and distillation, the alcoholic liquid is transferred to charred oak barrels and left to age and mellow for up to 15 years. The barrels have previously been used to mature bourbon in Kentucky and this is an important element that contributes to the unique flavours of this particular rum. While the rum matures in the barrels, it loses up to 7% by evaporation each year, so it is no surprise that the older rums are more valuable.

Open: *Monday to Friday, 9am–5pm. Saturday 10am–1pm.*
Time to allow: *¾ hour minimum.*
Facilities: *Gift shop. Toilets. Refreshments. Bar.*
Entrance Fee: *Bds$10. Children (under 12) free.*
Telephone: *425-9066*

Cockspur Rum Tour The other distillery on the island, the West India Rum Refinery, produce Cockspur rum. They have a tour each Wednesday when visitors can see around their distillation plant as well as the other stages in the process of producing the drink. The tour costs Bds$55 and includes a Bajan buffet lunch, live steel band, unlimited drinks and transport from/to your hotel, plus a sample bottle of Cockspur rum. Telephone 435-6900 for reservations.

ST NICHOLAS ABBEY (PLANTATION HOUSE)

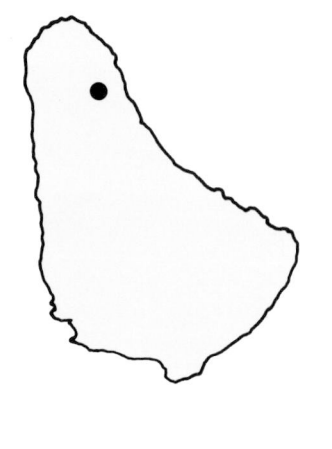

An unusual and interesting feature of the house is its chimneys and fireplaces – probably a legacy of its English ancestry.

A unique feature of a visit to St Nicholas Abbey is the remarkable 20 minute film taken in 1934. The film lay forgotten in a drawer for 45 years until discovered by the present owner, Lieutenant-Colonel Stephen Cave. Filmed by his father, it shows the family on a voyage to Barbados from England, the sugar plantation, windmills turning and street scenes in Bridgetown. The film is shown twice daily at 11.30am and 2.30pm.

St Nicholas Abbey is one of the oldest houses in the English speaking Western Hemisphere still in its near original condition, the others being Bacon's Castle in Virginia and Drax Hall in Barbados (not open to the public).

This Jacobean-style house was built around 1650-60 by Benjamin Berringer. The second owner, Sir John Yeamans, who acquired the property (and the previous owner's wife) by foul means, went on to become Governor of South Carolina in 1672. However the plantation takes its name from a later owner, George Nicholas, who married Berringer's grand-daughter. Today it is owned by the Cave family who acquired it in 1820 and from around that time the house has been known as St Nicholas Abbey although it was never an Abbey nor had any religious connections. It has always been a working sugar plantation.

There is a guided tour of the house, but as it is lived in, only the ground floor is open to the public. It is furnished with late 18th and early 19th century antiques. The short driveway up to the house is through a fine avenue of mahogany trees.

Open: *Monday to Friday, 10am–3.30pm.*
Time to allow: *½ hour (plus 20 minutes to see the film).*
Facilities: *Small gift shop. Toilets. Soft drinks available.*
Entrance Fee: *Bds$5.*
Telephone: *422-8725*

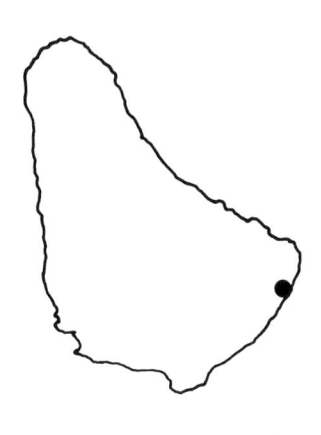

The four corners of the house face the four points of the compass.

Sam Lord's Castle was built by the notorious Samuel Hall Lord in the 1820s and is one of the finest mansions in Barbados, in Regency style and castellated. The Castle stands on 72 acres of land, and is today the Reception and centre-piece of Marriott's luxury hotel resort. The fine architecture, plaster work ceilings, chandeliers, massive gilded mirrors and period furniture have all been restored and maintained. Over the years a fine collection of pictures has been added, including works by Raeburn, Kneller, Reynolds and Lely.

The grounds and the castle's drawing room and dining room are open to visitors. The resort has some fine beaches where the Atlantic surf rolls in, but the sea can be dangerous for swimming – ask for advice.

Many words and songs have been written about Sam Lord (1778-1844). Legend has it that at night he hung lanterns in the coconut trees so that passing mariners thought they had reached the safe port of Bridgetown. As the ships attempted to approach the land they ran aground on the treacherous reefs and would then be looted. Certainly the nearby Cobblers Reef claimed many ships over the years (even after the building of lighthouses at South Point in 1852 and Ragged Point in 1875), however there has never been any firm evidence that Sam Lord did this, though he was a noted rogue.

Open to the public: *Daily (including week-ends), 8.30am–5pm.*
Facilities: *Hotel facilities. Shops (including a branch of "Best of Barbados") by the entrance to the grounds.*
Entrance Fee to Grounds: *Bds$7. Free entry for Barbadians on Sundays.*
Telephone: *423-7350*

SUNBURY PLANTATION HOUSE

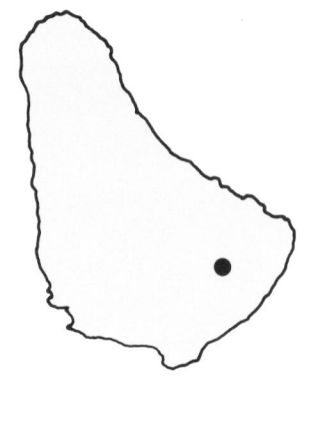

The grand entrance to Sunbury Plantation House.

This is not only a very old plantation house but unusual in that visitors have access to all the rooms. Sunbury was lived in until very recently. The present owners have retained the period furniture throughout the house and have also collected a large and fascinating range of additional Barbadian artifacts and memorabilia that are displayed in the rooms.

In the expansive cellars there is a museum with a diverse collection of items from past plantation life and is the finest agricultural exhibition on the island. There is also a unique display of horse-drawn carriages.

The present house is of uncertain age, and though the sugar plantation dates back to 1660 the house is probably from the early 1700s with later additions. From around 1777 it became known as Sunbury, named after the then owner's estate in England.

In 1981 the house was separated from the sugar plantation and is now privately owned and surrounded by spacious gardens. You can really savour grand living by having evening dinner in the house, seated at the 200 year old mahogany dining table.

The gift shop sells locally made handicrafts.

Open: *Daily (including week-ends), 10am–4.30pm.*
Time to allow: *1 hour minimum.*
Facilities: *Gift shop. Toilets. Restaurant.*
Note: *Evening dinners by prior reservation only.*
Entrance Fee: *Bds$8. Children (under 12) half price.*
Telephone: *423-6270*

VILLA NOVA (PLANTATION HOUSE)

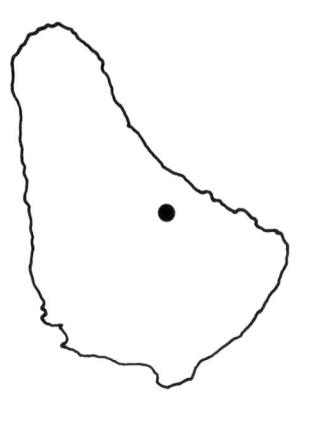

Villa Nova remains essentially as it was when built over 150 years ago.

This attractive sugar plantation house was built in 1834 by Mr Edmund Haynes of the Haynes family that once owned many estates on the island. Villa Nova ("new country house") was built just after the disastrous hurricane of 1831 which destroyed the original building (and most others on the island too).

As the house is lived in on occasions, only the ground floor public rooms can be viewed by visitors. Although the furniture is not original to the house, it is locally made antique mahogany furniture from the 19th century. The house incorporates many features of Barbadian great houses of that period, including the wide verandah, window shutters and parapet. The parapet was intended to protect the roof from hurricanes.

The house is surrounded by 6 acres of lovely landscaped gardens and woods that are full of wild orchids, flowering shrubs and trees and tropical fruit trees. Due to its elevation (800 feet, 240m, above sea level) and refreshing breeze, the temperature at Villa Nova can often be 9-10°F (5°C) lower than at sea level.

The sugar estates once extended to about one thousand acres (four hundred hectares) but in 1907 the house and 6½ acres were sold to the government to be used as the residence of the parish Medical Officer. From 1965 to 1971 the late Lord Avon (as Sir Anthony Eden, he was Prime Minister of Britain) and his wife Clarissa (a niece of Winston Churchill) owned Villa Nova for use as their winter home. During this time they entertained HM Queen Elizabeth II and Prince Philip to lunch. The house is still privately owned.

Open: *Monday to Friday, 9am–4pm.*
Time to allow: *½ hour minimum.*
Facilities: *Toilets. No refreshments. No shop.*
Entrance Fee: *Bds$8. Children (under 12) half price.*
Telephone: *433-1524*

Welchman Hall Gully

WELCHMAN HALL GULLY

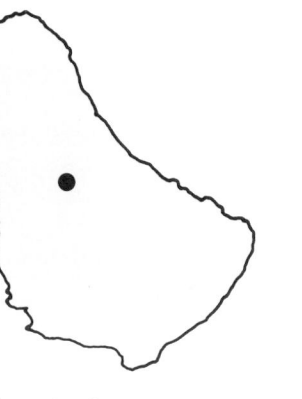

The path winds through a more open part of the gully.

When the first settlers landed in 1627, the whole island was covered in thick dense forest. Today it is difficult to visualise this as the trees were nearly all felled within a few decades to make way for sugar. Only small areas of forest survived, usually in gullies where sugar cane could not be grown.

To preserve at least a small portion of the island's past landscape, Welchman Hall Gully was acquired by the Barbados National Trust in 1962. It was originally part of Welchman Hall Plantation, and it is thought that the name arose because the original owner, a General Williams, was Welsh. It is a tranquil, easygoing ¾ mile (1.2km) walk from one end of the gully to the other along coralstone paths and up and down coralstone steps. One section has been kept as original, while in other sections there has been additional planting so there is a wide range of trees and tropical plants to see – including a grove of nutmeg trees, the macaw palm, bamboo, ficus trees, the cohune nut palm and the only clove tree on the island. The trees and plants are named and a number corresponds to that given in a Bds$1 leaflet which gives more information.

The gully makes a good habitat for monkeys and if you are quiet you may see them, especially in the early morning or late afternoon.

Along the gully sides are coralstone caves with stalagmites and stalactites, a reminder of the geological construction of this part of the island, and akin to the underground views in Harrison's Cave, part of which actually runs below this gully.

At the car park there are steps up to a viewpoint looking towards the Atlantic. If you are coming by taxi, you could ask to be dropped at the southern end entrance and be picked up at the car park at the northern end of the gully.

Open: *Daily (including week-ends), 9am–5pm.*
Time to allow: *1 hour minimum.*
Facilities: *Toilets at northern end. No refreshments. No shop.*
Note: *Path not suitable for baby pushchairs or wheelchairs.*
Entrance Fee: *Bds$5. Children (under 12) half price, (under 6) free.*
Telephone: *438-6671 (National Trust HQ: 426-2421 or 436-9033)*

OTHER THINGS TO SEE & DO

Bajan Sky Tours (Airport) The Barbados Light Aeroplane Club (tel: 428-4359) can offer a 30-minute aerial tour of the island in a Cessna light aircraft for Bds$130. The price includes transport from your hotel or cruise liner and a complimentary drink after the flight.

Banks Brewery (Wildey) The island's award-winning brewery offers free tours. For reservations, tel: 429-2113.

Bussa Statue (ABC H'way) Karl Broodhagen's impressive statue *(right)* commemorates the 150th anniversary of emancipation from slavery and is popularly known as the "Bussa Statue" after one of the leaders of the slave uprising in 1816. It stands on the roundabout where H'way 5 crosses the ABC Highway.

Cherry Tree Hill (St Andrew) There are superb views towards the south-east over St Andrew and the east coast from the road between St Nicholas Abbey and Morgan Lewis Mill.

Christ Church Parish Church (Oistins) The present church dates only from 1935, but is the fourth on that site, each previous one having been destroyed by hurricane or fire. The churchyard contains the famous Chase Vault where coffins mysteriously moved around within the sealed vault in the early 1800s. The coffins were removed and the vault is no longer used.

Cotton Tower Signal Station (St Joseph) Part of the same signal station chain as Gun Hill and Grenade Hall and similar in design to the latter. This National Trust property can be seen from the road but is currently not open to the public.

Dauntless Tomb (St Matthias Churchyard, Christ Church) This tomb is a memorial to the crew of *HM Screw Frigate Dauntless* who died of yellow fever, which broke out at sea on leaving St Thomas in the Virgin Islands in November 1852. 16 officers, 58 men and 11 boys perished (some at sea and the rest after arriving in Barbados) and it was not until March 1853 that the ship with her surviving crew were able to sail home.

Folkestone Marine Museum (Holetown) Temporarily closed to facilitate development of the new "Coastal & Marine Interpretive Centre" by the NCC (National Conservation Commission).

George Washington's House (Bush Hill House) George Washington visited Barbados in 1751, accompanying his half brother Lawrence, who was suffering from tuberculosis. Although a house in Bay Street is known as Washington House, it wasn't even built in 1751! Bush Hill House is in fact where the Washingtons stayed. The house subsequently became part of the military garrison area. (Not open to the public.)

Graeme Hall Swamp (Christ Church)   The last remaining mangrove swamp on the island and of ever decreasing size. A habitat for various flora and fauna, including the white cattle egrets that return here to roost each sunset.

Hackleton's Cliff (St John)   There is a commanding view from the cliff top with its elevation of about 1,000ft (300m). There is now a good road (a cul-de-sac) to the cliff and you can park near the cliff top.

Harmony Hall (St Michael)   A historic house and fine example of early Barbadian 18th century architecture. Now the headquarters of the Barbados Workers Union.

Military Cemetery (near Hilton Hotel)   Dating from the early 19th century and still is use today for those who have served in the military. Recently restored.

National Art Collection   There is at present no permanent home for this collection.

Observatory (Clapham, St Michael)   Named after the co-founder of the Barbados Astronomical Society, the Harry Bayley Observatory is equipped with a 14 inch reflector telescope and is open to the public every Friday from 8.30pm. It is well worth a visit.

Oistins   This is the main town on the south coast. Known chiefly as the island's fishing port it has a new fish market. Scene for the annual Oistins Fish Festival. Historically important as the site where in 1652 the treaty was signed ending the civil war between the Barbadian Royalists and the Parliamentary forces.

Petrea Gardens (St James)   These recently created gardens are located on a small back road, running parallel to H'way 1, between Porters and Trents. This oasis of greenery features a lake and waterfall. Visitors welcome.

St George's Church   The present building *(left)* dates from 1784 and is the oldest church on the island. Its altar painting (1776) is by the famous painter, Benjamin West, who was the only American to become President of the Royal Academy. The centurion in his picture has had a black patch placed over an eye reputedly punched out by a thief who thought he was being watched by the centurion.

St John's Church   The present church dates from 1836, its predecessors having succumbed to hurricanes. From the grounds there are fine views and in the churchyard is the grave of Ferdinand Paleologus, the last collateral descendent of the Christian Emperor of Constantinople, Constantine VIII, who was murdered in 1453. Paleologus emigrated to Barbados via England and died here in 1678.   (Note: Drinks available in the church shop).

St Peter's Church   The present parish church of St Peter, located in Speightstown, dates from 1837 but was severely damaged by fire in 1980 and has since been rebuilt.

There is an excellent book titled "Historic Churches of Barbados" by Barbara Hill, edited by Henry Fraser.

OTHER THINGS TO SEE & DO

Satellite Earth Station (St John) This large satellite dish belongs to Barbados External Communications and gives the island its excellent telephone and fax links with the rest of the world. (Not open to the public but clearly visible if driving in that part of the island).

Sharon Moravian Church (Near Jackson, St Thomas) An interesting building architecturally and historically important because the Moravians were the first missionaries who set out (in the mid 18th century) to bring Christianity and education *solely* to the slaves.

South Point Lighthouse *(Right)* This is the oldest in Barbados, dating from 1852 and is made entirely of iron, prefabricated and bolted together.

Speightstown *(Left)* Historically it was sometimes called Little Bristol due to its trade links with Bristol in England. It is the island's second town and named after William Speight who originally owned the land there. See also the entry on St Peter's Church on the previous page.

Turner's Hall Wood (St Andrews) This is a small but unique part of Barbados as it is virtually the only section of the island left with original forest. When the first English settlers landed they cut down the trees that covered the whole island in order to plant crops and used the cut wood as fuel. Turner's Hall Wood is a bit isolated and is best only visited with someone who is familiar with the area. (A part of Welchman Hall Gully also has near original forest).

Tyrol Cot (St Michael) The home of the late Sir Grantley Adams, first Premier of Barbados and birthplace of his son, Tom Adams, who became Prime Minister. The house itself is of considerable architectural interest. Now currently under restoration by the Barbados National Trust and due to be opened to the public in due course as a major visitor attraction.

Wind-generator If driving in St Lucy you may notice a large modern windmill. This is operated by the Barbados Light & Power Company and generates electricity ■

SIGHTSEEING TOURS

Tour No1: "Around The Island"

Tour No2: Scenic

Tour No3: Flora & Fauna

Tour No4: Historic

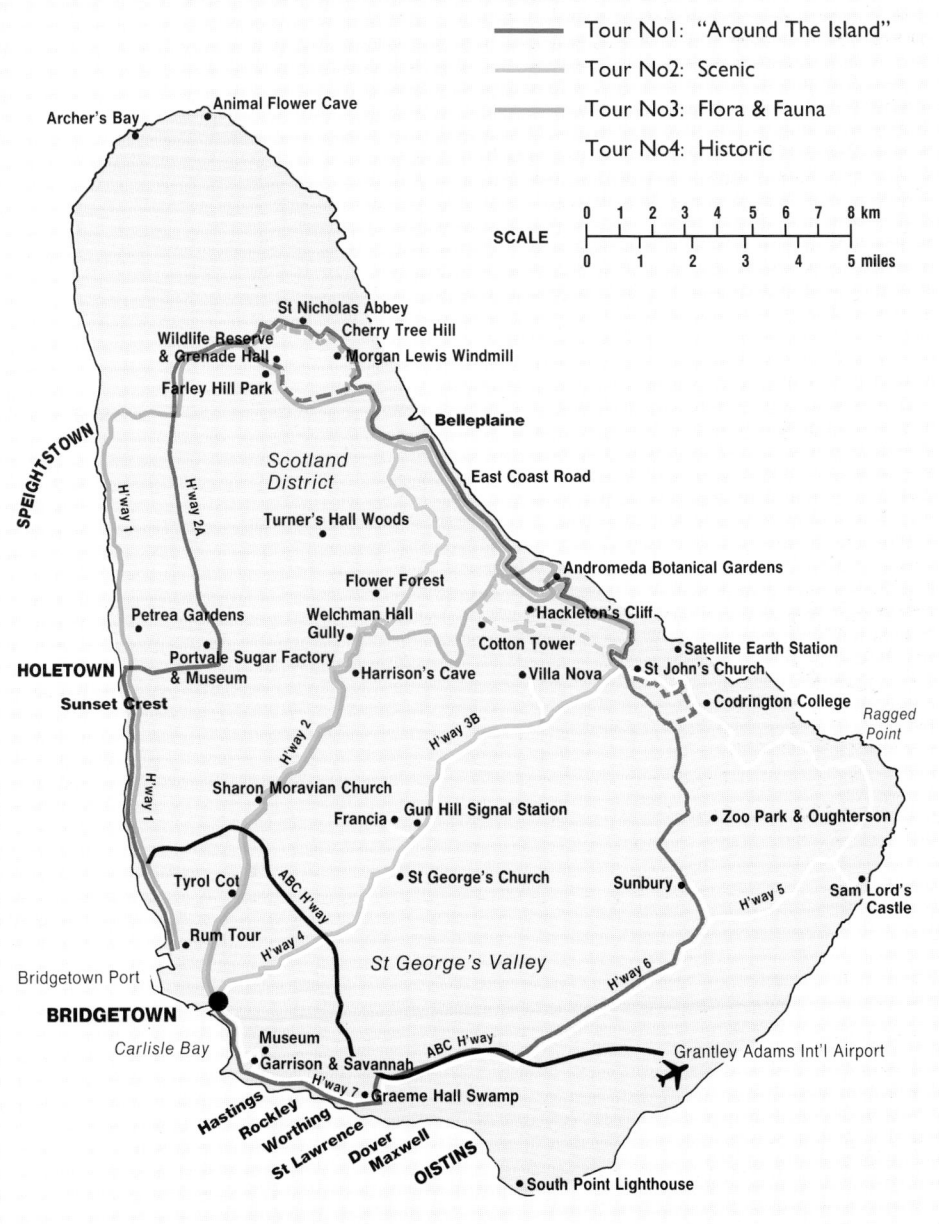

There are four suggested tours on the following pages. Each is indicated on the map above. These tours by taxi or self-drive car will all take a full day and require an early start if you want to spend ample time at the different locations en route. Although all tours start and end nominally in Bridgetown centre, with the ABC Highway it is easy to adapt the routes for starting from either the West or South coast.   **Note:** Attractions highlighted in **bold letters** on the following pages are described in the previous chapter.

SIGHTSEEING TOUR No1: "AROUND THE ISLAND"

Relevant Attractions En Route:

Rum Tour
Holetown
Portvale Sugar Factory & Sugar Museum
St Nicholas Abbey (Plantation House)
Cherry Tree Hill (view)
Morgan Lewis Sugar Windmill
East Coast Road
Andromeda Botanical Gardens
St John's Church (& view)
Sunbury Plantation House
Bridgetown Centre (& shopping)

Optional Attractions:

Barbados Wildlife Reserve & Grenade Hall
Farley Hill Park
Codrington College
Barbados Zoo Park
    (& Oughterson Plantation House)
Garrison Savannah & Barbados Museum

This is a very comprehensive tour of the island but fairly demanding and lengthy as there is a lot to see and you will need to choose which attractions you prefer.

Suggested Route: A good starting point is the **Rum Tour** at Mount Gay as their short audio-visual presentation covers the island's history and the importance of sugar and rum. Then head north up the west coast highway (H'way 1) to **Holetown** where the original settlers landed. In Holetown, turn right up H'way 1A heading inland until you meet the junction with H'way 2A at St Thomas' Parish Church. Turn left and within about ⅓rd mile (½ km) you will see, on the left, **Portvale Sugar Factory** (and the Sir Frank Hutson Sugar Museum). From there, continue northwards up H'way 2A to the village of Mile and a Quarter, and bear right up the hill until you join the new H'way 1 at a T-junction. Turn right and about ⅔rd mile (1km) later bear left to **St Nicholas Abbey**, **Cherry Tree Hill** and **Morgan Lewis Windmill**. If you prefer, keep on the main highway to take the optional route via the **Barbados Wildlife Reserve**, **Grenade Hall** and **Farley Hill Park**.

Whichever route you choose, you will ultimately wind your way downhill to St Andrew's Parish Church and then the village of Belleplaine. In Belleplaine turn left onto the **East Coast Road** with its lovely views out across the Atlantic. At the southern end by Cattlewash, the road passes a number of holiday houses and then turns inland. You climb away from the coast then come to a junction, where you join H'way 3 going south-east to **Andromeda Botanical Gardens**. Look out for the left signpost to these beautiful gardens.

From Andromeda head south-east before the road climbs up to **St John's Church**. From the church you can either head south-east via Colleton or take the optional route towards **Codrington College**. Note this road becomes quite steep with sharp bends. You can see the **Satellite Earth Station** clearly.

With either route you eventually pass close to the **Barbados Zoo Park** at Oughterson. Now head down H'way 4B until St Philip's Parish Church where you turn left to **Sunbury Plantation House**. From Sunbury head to Six Cross Roads then south-west down H'way 6 until it reaches the ABC H'way at a roundabout. Join the ABC H'way but turn left off it at the 2nd roundabout, then turn right at the next roundabout. You will now be on the south coast road (H'way 7) heading back into Bridgetown. Back in Bridgetown you pass the historic **Garrison & Savannah**, with the **Barbados Museum** nearby.

Lunch/Snack: You can have a snack or lunch at the Sand Dunes snackette at Belleplaine (on the East Coast Road), the Kingsley Inn at Cattlewash, the Hibiscus Café at Andromeda Botanical Gardens or the restaurant at Sunbury Plantation House. (On the optional route, there are refreshments available at the Barbados Wildlife Reserve).

SIGHTSEEING TOUR No2: SCENIC

Relevant Attractions En Route:
Harrison's Cave
Flower Forest (& views)
East Coast Road
St John's Church (& view)
Gun Hill Signal Station (& view)

Optional Attractions:
Welchman Hall Gully
Andromeda Botanical Gardens
Cotton Tower & Hackleton's Cliff
Villa Nova (Plantation House)
Francia Plantation House

Barbados is a beautiful island and this tour will take you to see some of its finest scenery and views.

Suggested Route: From Bridgetown, head north-east across the island on H'way 2 towards Harrison's Cave. En route you pass the interesting **Sharon Moravian Church** and there are lovely views south (looking back) as you climb slowly uphill past Hopewell House.

The first major attraction on this route is **Harrison's Cave**. A tram ride through the cavernous underground halls is memorable (but you should book in advance). Further on there is the north entrance and car park of **Welchman Hall Gully**. For open scenic views towards the Atlantic combined with a walk through flowering undergrowth, shrubs and trees, head to the **Flower Forest**, which is set on a hillside.

From the Flower Forest, head towards Belleplaine on the picturesque road via Melvin Hill, the Saddle Back and Bissex. At Belleplaine turn right onto the **East Coast Road**. At the southern end by Cattlewash, the road passes a number of holiday houses and then turns inland. You climb away from the coast then come to a junction, where you can either join H'way 3 going south-east to **Andromeda Botanical Gardens** or head south-west up Horse Hill turning left past the **Cotton Tower Signal Station** to finally stop and enjoy the fabulous view from **Hackelton's Cliff**.

Whichever route you take, you will eventually come to **St John's Church**, then head south-west across the island on H'way 3B, turning off to see **Villa Nova**, if you so wish.

Continue on the highway to see **Gun Hill Signal Station** (note the small road to Gun Hill from the highway is a one-way road – watch the signs). If you want to detour to see nearby **Francia Plantation House** then you should head down the hill towards Bridgetown for about 1/3rd mile (1/2km), then turn right to Francia (indicated by small signs). Now head south-west back to the ABC H'way and home.

Lunch/Snack: You can have a snack or lunch at the Flower Forest, the Sand Dunes snackette at Belleplaine (on the East Coast Road), the Kingsley Inn at Cattlewash or the Hibiscus Café at Andromeda Botanical Gardens.

Alternative Tour: This takes you to the very northern tip of the island. From **Welchman Hall Gully** or the **Flower Forest**, instead of going direct to Belleplaine, go first to Cattlewash then up the **East Coast Road**, through Belleplaine, past St Andrew's Parish Church and then either: a) drive up to **Morgan Lewis Windmill**, enjoy the view from **Cherry Tree Hill** and see **St Nicholas Abbey**, or b) route via **Farley Hill** and the **Barbados Wildlife Reserve & Grenade Hall**. Either way, join H'way 1 and beyond the roundabout at St Lucy's Parish Church take H'way 1C going to the **Animal Flower Cave**. Then route back south to Bridgetown via the west coast highway (H'way 1) or the inland road (H'way 2A).

SIGHTSEEING TOUR No3: FLORA & FAUNA

Relevant Attractions En Route:
Welchman Hall Gully
Flower Forest
Andromeda Botanical Gardens
East Coast Road
Farley Hill Park
Barbados Wildlife Reserve
& Grenade Hall Forest

Optional Attractions:
Harrison's Cave
Morgan Lewis Sugar Windmill
Cherry Tree Hill (view)
St Nicholas Abbey (Plantation House)
Speightstown
Holetown
Rum Tour

This tour takes you to some of the island's finest gardens and parks open to the public where you can see a profusion of tropical plants, shrubs and trees in addition to wildlife. Note: The tour does involve quite a bit of walking to get the most from it.

Suggested Route: From Bridgetown, head north-east across the island on H'way 2 towards Welchman Hall Gully. There are lovely views south (looking back) as you climb slowly uphill past Hopewell House. En route you pass the entrance road to **Harrison's Cave** (which you should book in advance if you want to see it). The car park and northern entrance to **Welchman Hall Gully** is further on. The gully is full of interesting trees and shrubs and it is an easy walk. A short distance to the east is the **Flower Forest** which is a great place for flower lovers with its flowering undergrowth, shrubs and trees.

From the Flower Forest continue east via Coffee Gully, H'way 3 and Horse Hill (quite steep downhill) towards **Andromeda Botanical Gardens**. Look out for the left signpost to these beautiful gardens.

From the Andromeda car park, turn right and head along the coast road loop which eventually goes inland and uphill then after a couple of junctions starts downhill once more to Cattlewash and the **East Coast Road**. Look out for the interesting *Maypole Agave* which is common in this area. At the T-junction in Belleplaine, turn right, then right again at St Andrew's Parish Church. At the next major junction you can either travel via H'way 2 to **Farley Hill Park** and the **Barbados Wildlife Reserve & Grenade Hall Forest**, or take a right turn to go past **Morgan Lewis Windmill**, enjoy the view from **Cherry Tree Hill** and see **St Nicholas Abbey**.

Either way you will end up on H'way 1 heading west. Turn left towards the village of Mile and a Quarter, where you bear left to get onto H'way 2A heading south. In about ⅞th mile (1.4km) turn right towards **Speightstown** via The Whim. This road takes you through an attractive little gully before you get to Speightstown, where you turn left at the Bus Terminal traffic lights.

Now head back home on the west coast highway (H'way 1) through **Holetown**. Finally, you may like to stop at the Mount Gay Visitor Centre on the Spring Garden Highway for a **Rum Tour**.

Lunch/Snack: You can have a snack or lunch at the Flower Forest, the Hibiscus Café at Andromeda Botanical Gardens, the Bonito Bar or the Atlantis Hotel at Bathsheba (shortly after you leave Andromeda), the Kingsley Inn at Cattlewash, the Sand Dunes snackette at Belleplaine (on the East Coast Road) or at the Barbados Wildlife Reserve.

See Also: If you have the time on another day, the two plantation great houses of **Francia** and **Villa Nova** have nice gardens that are worth visiting. There is also the nature trail and grounds at **Codrington College**. For those interested in animals, there is the **Barbados Zoo Park** at Oughterson. For bird lovers there is **Graeme Hall Swamp**. From Jan-Apr on Wednesdays there is the **National Trust Open House** (and gardens) programme.

SIGHTSEEING TOUR No4: HISTORIC

Relevant Attractions En Route:

The Garrison & Savannah
Barbados Museum
Sunbury Plantation House
    (with its agricultural museum)
Sam Lord's Castle
Codrington College
St John's Church (& view)
Villa Nova (Plantation House)
Gun Hill Signal Station (& view)
Francia Plantation House

Optional Attraction:

Bridgetown Centre

This tour will give you some idea of the history of Barbados as well as being a most interesting and entertaining excursion.

Suggested Route: From the city centre, head down Bay Street, turning sharp left onto the Garrison Road (so the **Garrison Savannah** is on your right hand side). You will pass the Main Guard and the Cannon Collection en route to the **Barbados Museum**, which is housed in what was the military jail. On leaving the Museum, return to the south coast road (H'way 7) and turn left heading east. As you pass St Lawrence you come to a major round-about, turn left and then right at the next roundabout onto the ABC H'way (heading east).

Two roundabouts later, turn left onto H'way 6 heading for Six Cross Roads. From there, head north up to **Sunbury Plantation House** (look out for the signs). From Sunbury return to Six Cross Roads and head east on H'way 5 until turning right towards **Sam Lord's Castle**, a 19th century mansion with splendid interior, now the centre-piece of a luxury resort. From Sam Lord's return to H'way 5 then route towards **Codrington College** via the rugged eastern tip of the island. From here, head north-west to **St John's Church**, which is perched on a cliff top with commanding views. Note the road becomes quite steep with sharp bends. You can see the **Satellite Earth Station** clearly.

From St John's Church, head south-west on H'way 3B, detouring via the plantation great house of **Villa Nova**. After Villa Nova, return to H'way 3B and continue on to **Gun Hill Signal Station** (note the small road to Gun Hill from the highway is a one-way road – watch the signs). After Gun Hill, if you want to see nearby **Francia Plantation House** then you should head down the hill towards Bridgetown for about 1/3rd mile (1/2km), then turn right to Francia (indicated by small signs). Before heading back to the city, nearby there is the historic **St George's Church** with its altar painting by Benjamin West.

On returning to the city, there are a number of historic buildings which may interest you, if you still have the energy after a long day's tour. Refer to the **Bridgetown Centre** entry earlier in this book.

Lunch/Snack: You can have a snack or lunch at Sunbury Plantation House or Sam Lord's Castle. None of the subsequent locations out that way has a café or restaurant, although there is Tony-Anne's Restaurant and bar near Francia on the return leg of your journey.

See Also: If you have time on another day, there is the **Sir Frank Hutson Sugar Museum** by **Portvale Sugar Factory**, **Morgan Lewis Windmill**, the 1934 ciné film that can be seen at **St Nicholas Abbey** and the recently restored **Grenade Hall** ■

FESTIVALS & EVENTS

If you visit the island at the right time of year, it is worthwhile trying to see the following events (listed here in date order). For sporting events, see the next chapter.

Holetown Festival (one week in February) This commemorates the landing of the first settlers in February 1627 and was first held on the 350th anniversary of that event. It's a smaller and more local event than Crop Over but great fun nevertheless with musical entertainment, arts and crafts exhibitions, displays and a busy Saturday street fair. Look out for the distinctive Tuk band.

Annual Flower Show (one long week-end in February) Held at Balls Plantation, it is run by the Barbados Horticultural Society. The Flower Show includes displays from other tropical countries and usually the excellent Royal Barbados Police Band plays at the event.

Oistins Fish Festival (Easter) This festival has been running since 1978 and is a celebration of the island's fishing industry. There are demonstrations of fishing skills, races and competitions. Spectators can enjoy dancing to steel bands and admiring the arts and crafts exhibitions.

Easter Sunday Kite-Flying If you are in the island at Easter then head to the Garrison Savannah on Easter Sunday to see the annual kite-flying competition. It's spectacular and great fun for all the family.

Crop Over (July) This is the biggest festival, which as its name suggests, celebrates the end of the annual sugar-cane harvest. Although it is a very old festival with origins in the mid nineteenth century or even earlier, its present form dates from 1974. Even before Crop Over officially starts, calypsonians begin to compete with each other, culminating in the exciting Pic-O-De-Crop Calypso Finals at the National Stadium. There are also a host of other events happening around the island at this time. See the local press for details.

The colourful climax of Crop Over which takes place at the National Stadium.

Kadooment Day (First Monday in August) "Kadooment" is a Barbadian word meaning "an important event" and this is the climax of Crop Over. In the excited atmosphere of carnival, costumed bands parade at the National Stadium, then to the sounds of the latest calypsos they spend the day dancing their way to the Spring Garden Highway accompanied by large crowds (the highway is closed to traffic for the day). There is food, music and dancing until evening.

NIFCA (November) NIFCA stands for the National Independence Festival of Creative Arts. It was started in 1972 to encourage the island's creative arts, from school level upwards. It's a cultural festival which embraces drama, music, literature, painting, dance, culinary arts and photography, culminating on Independence Day.

Independence Day (30th November) A huge and colourful parade is held at the Garrison Savannah ■

SPORTS
& ACTIVITIES

Chapters in this Section:

Jill Walker

SPORTS & ACTIVITIES

For the more active visitor, Barbados offers a wide range of sports and activities besides sightseeing, shopping, sun-bathing and swimming . . . .

Athletics   There are athletic competitions, held usually at Whitsun, which attract athletes from home and abroad to compete in track and field events over several days. Such competitions are usually held at the National Stadium.

Cricket   Cricket is almost synonymous with the West Indies and Sunday village matches can be seen taking place all around the island. Barbados has produced some of the finest cricket players in the world. One of the best known is Sir Garfield Sobers who holds a number of cricketing records and is the game's greatest ever player. International Test matches take place at Kensington Oval in Bridgetown and are major events. Capacity crowds watch the game while the rest of the population follow the radio commentary intently.

Cricket match near Codrington College.
(East Point Lighthouse in the far distance).

Deep Sea Fishing   Fishing is an important island industry and depending on the season the seas abound with flying fish, marlin, barracuda, kingfish and dorado (the latter known locally as "dolphin"). If interested in doing some fishing yourself, visit the Careenage to select a boat for charter. It costs about Bds$500 per boat per half day, including drinks and snacks.

Flying   The Barbados Light Aeroplane Club is located on the southern side of the airport (tel: 428-4359) and has Cessna aircraft for hire (at Bds$130/hour) or tuition (Bds$170/hour). They are keen to offer flying training to visitors (who need to join the Club for Bds$50). If you just want to have an aerial tour of the island, this can be arranged too, including collection from your hotel or cruise liner.

Golf   There are at present four golf courses on the island – the 18 hole course at Sandy Lane (tel: 432-1145) and the 9 hole courses at Rockley Resort (tel: 435-7873), Heywoods Resort (tel: 422-4900) and the Bel Air Par 3 course (tel: 423-4653). A round will cost about Bds$30-90 + (for 9 holes) and clubs can be hired. Phone first to check the prices and to book. The new Royal Westmoreland course opens soon.

Hikes & Walks   The Barbados National Trust (tel: 436-9033) in conjunction with the Duke of Edinburgh Award Scheme, organises walks through the rural areas of the island. The walks are on Sundays and last about 3 hours, always starting at 6am before the sun gets too hot. There is also an afternoon walk and occasionally a moonlight one. Walks begin and end at the same point. There is a nominal Bds$3 charge and walkers are divided into groups depending on their fitness and interests so they can "stop and stare" or "hare and there"!

Horse Racing   The race track at the Garrison Savannah is the scene of exciting horse racing on a number of Saturdays during the racing season. The premier event is the Cockspur Gold Cup Race held each March and run over 9 furlongs. Horses from other Caribbean islands participate in this prestigious event. It is a colourful and fun occasion for all the family.

Horse Riding   There are a number of riding schools on the island offering both lessons and scenic trail rides for beginners and experienced riders. It costs about Bds$50-55 per hour. Some schools are listed in the Yellow Pages (under "Riding Academies") though there are others too. The Caribbean International Riding Centre in St Joseph (tel: 433-1453) offers Riding Holidays in addition to their professional horse riding training, dressage and jumping, for everyone from complete beginners to advanced riders (both children and adults).

Horse riding is a popular vacation pastime.

Motor Sports   There are a number of motor sports events held in Barbados, including international rallying. Circuit racing is carried out at Bushy Park in St Philip. For details, contact the Barbados Rally Club (tel: 426-0603).

Photo Tours   Keen photographers can join a 3½ hour "Photo Tour" by coach for Bds$80 which visits the picturesque Scotland district and east coast, stopping frequently en route. The alternative "Photo Safari" for Bds$60 goes to one off-the-beaten-track area. For details, tel: 426-0830.

Running   A number of 10K races and a 42K marathon are run in Barbados each year. The "Run Barbados" events are usually held in early December and attract well-known international runners from North America, Europe and the Caribbean. Taken almost as seriously, the annual "Fun Run" raises money for charity. Some 1,000 people participate and there are two distances – 4½ miles (7km) or 9 miles (14½km), to cater for different abilities.

Sailing/Yachting   The Caribbean is a fine place for sailing and yachting. There are two local clubs, the Barbados Cruising Club and the Barbados Yacht Club. These clubs have nice facilities and a super beach too. Several 40-60ft monohulls and catamarans are available for charter with skipper and crew from the Careenage. They can offer a range of sailings from lunch trips or sunset cruises to full day charters around the island. Costs are typically from Bds$100 per person for half a day, including food and drinks, but there may be a minimum size of party required. Smaller sailing boats, such as Hobie Cats, Zuma and Sunfish are available for hire from watersports operators – please refer to the next chapter.

Squash   There are a number of air-conditioned squash courts on the island. Contact the Barbados Squash Club (tel: 427-7913).

Swimming (Competition)   Barbados has a 50 metre, 10-lane swimming pool (plus a 25 metre training pool) at the Aquatic Centre in Wildey. Tel: 429-7946.

Tennis   Although several hotels have hard-surface tennis courts, these are normally only available to hotel residents. But there are public courts at Folkestone Park in Holetown.

Triathlon   The triathlon combines long-distance running, swimming and cycling. Held annually, this exciting and demanding event attracts athletes from the Caribbean and further afield.

In addition to the above list of sports and activities, there are many others too: Basketball, Bodybuilding, Boxing, Badminton, Bridge, Chess, Clay Pigeon Shooting, Cycling, Darts, Dominoes, Draughts, Football, Hockey, Judo, Karate, Karting, Netball, Polo, Rifle & Pistol Shooting, Rugby, Table Tennis, Volley Ball etc. . .   For information on any of these, you could try the National Sports Council at Blenheim, St Michael. Tel: 436-6127.

In 1993 the new indoor gymnasium *(left)*, built by the Chinese, was opened at Wildey, beside the Aquatic Centre.

Barbados offers a very comprehensive range of watersports with expert tuition catering for both complete novices and those who are experienced. The seas and reefs around the island provide an excellent and varied environment ranging from the placid Caribbean off the west and south coasts to the wilder Atlantic off the eastern side of the island.

Many hotels have their own watersports facilities and there are in addition several independent watersports operators. These are: Blue Reef Water Sports at Glitter Bay (tel: 422-3133); Pakis Watersports at Grand Barbados Beach Resort (tel: 426-9947); the Watersports Centre at The Barbados Hilton (tel: 436-3549) and Willie's Watersports at several locations (tel: 432-5980).

Glass Bottom Boating If you don't want to snorkel or scuba dive, then a Glass Bottom Boat offers an easy way to see the marine life around the inshore coral reefs. Look out for these boats on the west or south coasts. A trip costs approximately Bds$15.

Jet skiing These high-speed water scooters are available for hire from operators for around Bds$40 for a 20 minute ride. Be careful to keep outside swimming and snorkelling areas and don't try riding a jet ski if you have been drinking.

Para Sailing If you have a head for heights, then strap on a parachute and be towed up to around 200ft by a motor-boat. Contact Skyranger Parasail at Holetown Beach (tel: 452-2323). A flight costs Bds$60 for a 10 minute trip.

Sailing Small but nimble dinghies (Sunfish or Zuma) suitable for one or two people are available for individual hire from several operators for Bds$25-40/hour. Don't be tempted to stray too far out to sea as the winds blow offshore and the next land-fall (St Lucia or St Vincent) is rather far away! Alternatively you can crew or just enjoy a sail on a fast catamaran (Hobie Cats) that are usually skippered and cost about Bds$30-40 per ½ hour.

Snorkelling This is best off the west and south coasts. There are coral reefs within yards of the beach so you need not swim far out. Equipment can be hired for about Bds$15 per hour or purchased locally. Keep a watch out for Jet Skis and speedboats that often come close inshore and it is wise to use a marker float to warn others of your presence. Avoid any stone fish or moray eel you might encounter.

Sub-aqua (Scuba Diving) With sunshine the year round, crystal clear water with visibility sometimes up to 100ft (30m) and the water temperature around 78°F (25°C) – this all helps to make Barbados an ideal dive location for both beginners and experts. Add to that the presence of abundant marine life, inshore reefs and wrecks at shallow depths and expert tuition. There is even a decompression chamber on the island.

Several operators in Barbados offer expert tuition (full PADI and NAUI certification courses are available). Beginners are actively encouraged. Mike and Sandy Seale of Exploresub Barbados (tel: 435-6542) operate the only PADI Five-Star training facility on the island. Mike has been diving for over 21 years and is a Master-Scuba Diver trainer. With Exploresub Barbados' experienced and qualified team they can offer everything from a one day course for non-divers designed to get you diving that day, to complete 7-14 day dive packages. They have a full range of equipment for hire including cameras and video for underwater photography. A nice idea is their special underwater rendezvous they can

Diving on the French tug "Berwyn" which sunk in Carlisle Bay in 1919.

arrange with the Atlantis submarine on which they will book (at a 20% discount) your non-dive friends and family.

Remember to ask Mike about George, the amazing dancing Barracuda who inhabits the wreck of the *SS Stavronikita*.

Another sub-aqua operator is Willie's Watersports (tel:432-5980), who can also offer other watersports such as water-skiing, sailing, windsurfing and jet-ski hire. There is also Dive Safari (tel: 427-4350) and the Dive Shop (tel: 426-9947).

Surfing   This is a popular local sport when surf conditions are right. The usual places are Bathsheba or the Crane though surfing can sometimes be seen at other locations. Both national and international events are held.

Swimming   See separate entry BEACHES, over the page.

Water Skiing   Many people try their first water skiing while visiting the island – the warm water being most welcome if you fall in, which is usually frequent as a learner. Contact any of the watersports' operators.   Costs are typically: Bds$30 for 15 minutes.

Windsurfing   The constant trade winds that blow during the winter months combined with warm seas make Barbados an ideal location for windsurfing and several international events have been held here. Windsurfing is normally done off the southwest and west coasts for novices and the south coast for more experienced windsurfers as the seas and wind become distinctly more challenging as you move closer to the Atlantic side of the island.

Boards are available for hire from several operators, such as the Windsurfing Club (tel: 428-7277) Silverrock Windsurfing Rentals on (tel: 428-2866), Silver Sands Resort on (tel: 428-6001) and Willie's Watersports on (tel: 443-5980). Windsurfer hire costs are about Bds$20-30 per hour.

Caution When you are on the beach you may be approached by watersports operators. Note the prices they quote may be in US Dollars rather than Barbados Dollars, so remember to clarify this point.

Danger There are dangerous currents around the north and east coasts. Don't surf or swim there without local advice ∎

BEACHES

Barbados has many fine, white coral, sandy beaches – one of the island's attractive features. Below the high-water mark all beaches are open to the public but above the mark may be private property and any sunloungers you may see are usually meant only for hotel residents. Beaches are never crowded as in Mediterranean resorts but are busier at week-ends and on public holidays.

Generally, the waters that lap the west and south-west coasts are calm and the beaches slope gently into the sea. Very occasionally there can be tricky currents that your hotel may warn you about. At certain times of the year, shoals of small jellyfish stray close to the beach but apart from a sting they are harmless. If there is no one else already swimming, take care. The south-east coast has rougher seas with larger rollers suitable for body surfing. The eastern coast is not recommended for swimming as it is very dangerous.

Barbados is blessed with many beaches but some of them are isolated and it is probably imprudent for lone tourists to use them, particularly as there are so many other lovely beaches to choose from, for example . . . .

Alleynes Bay (West Coast)   A typical fine west coast beach by the Colony Club Hotel. At the northern end are some reefs that are popular for snorkelling.

Carlisle Bay (South-West Coast)   The main bathing area is at the southern end near to the Yacht and Cruising Clubs and the hotels. Watersports are usually available.

Cattlewash (East Coast)   The East Coast Road runs alongside this huge expanse of beach with its exhilarating sea-breeze. See also the entry in BEST THINGS TO SEE & DO. Super for beach walks and to dip in the rock pools but definitely not suitable for swimming. For the expert surfer there is the "Soup Bowl" at Bathsheba where championships are held.

Crane Beach (South-East Coast)   A very quiet though attractive beach below the Crane Beach Hotel. There is a small charge for access via the hotel but this is refundable when you purchase a meal or drink and is well worthwhile to enjoy the ambience of this resort and its stunning location. Note: The sea can be dangerous for swimming – ask for advice.

Dover Beach (South-West Coast)   Off St Lawrence Gap, this beach has bars and restaurants nearby. Watersports are usually available.

Heywoods Beach/Six Men's Bay (West Coast)   This is a long beach with easy access from the northern end and parking beside the beach. Suitable for swimming and snorkelling. Watersports are usually available from the beach near to the resort itself.

Maxwell Beach/Casuarina Beach (South-West Coast)   Off the Maxwell Coast Road, this is a popular beach with a good breeze offshore for intermediate windsurfers.

Miami Beach (South-West Coast)   Also called Enterprise Beach. Sheltered to some extent from the prevailing trade winds.

Mullins Beach (West Coast)   A popular beach beside the road with the well-known Mullins Beach Bar alongside. Gibbs Beach lies to the south.

Paynes Bay (West Coast)   Public access is at the northern end of the bay. Road side parking available. Snorkelling at the north end. Watersports are usually available. You can walk along the beach to Sandy Lane.

Rockley Beach (South-West Coast)   Also called Accra Beach. This is a busy popular beach and has lockers and permanent beach vendors stalls. Various watersports activities are usually available.

Sam Lord's Castle (South-East Coast)   Access via Sam Lord's Castle (see that entry in the chapter BEST THINGS TO SEE & DO). A nice beach below the cliffs – but be careful of the large rollers! The sea can be dangerous for swimming – ask for advice.

Sandy Lane (West Coast)   This beach is in front of the prestigious Sandy Lane Hotel. You can access the beach via Paynes Bay (see above). Watersports are usually available.

Silver Sands (South-East Coast)   This is the main location for windsurfing, but it is considered too breezy for complete beginners.

Worthing Beach/Sandy Beach (South-West Coast)   A lagoon-type bay situated to the east of Accra Beach and not quite so busy.

CAUTIONS

Sunburn   Remember Barbados is a mere 13^0 above the equator and the sun will burn! The breeze may make you feel cool but take care as the sun is particularly strong from as early as 10am to as late as 3-4pm. Do wear sunblock, a sun hat and even a T-shirt over your swimsuit if you are swimming for a long time. Remember that swimming gradually washes away sun block lotions, so reapply regularly. The reflected light from the water and the sand will also intensify your rate of burning. If you do get sunburnt you could try *aloe vera* – a succulent plant. The yellow juice from a leaf squeezed onto the burn will have a soothing effect.

Sea urchins (Sea eggs)   These usually live on the rocks below the water. The two most common types are either black or white. The black ones have long, fragile spines that are apt to break off painfully in your foot if you happen to stand on one whilst swimming. The remedies include drawing the spines out with candle wax (don't just pull them out). Your hotel should know how to help, but probably a visit to the doctor will be necessary. The white sea eggs have short spines and are harmless. Their flesh is eaten as a traditional delicacy.

Coral   Be careful not to graze yourself on coral as the wound is not only painful but it will also not heal readily.

Manchineel Trees   These grow at the edge of some beaches. The small green apple-like fruits are poisonous. Do not shelter under the tree if it rains as the washed-down sap can irritate the skin.

Beach vendors   Official beach vendors operate from fixed stalls and wear light blue jackets with yellow lapels. They sell beachwear, plait hair etc. Unofficial vendors roam the beaches with briefcases full of trinkets to sell, and can be a nuisance if all you want is peace and quiet. They will normally respect your wishes if you say "no thank-you" politely but firmly.

Life-guards   Where there is a life-guard station, do heed the flags. A red flag means keep out of the water, an orange flag means there is danger due to strong currents and tides and a green flag signifies that it is safe for swimming.

Security   It is wise never to leave valuables unattended on the beach. Topless sun-bathing or swimming is not permitted though seen on occasions. Beware of predatory "beach bums" ■

VISITS TO OTHER ISLANDS

While staying in Barbados you might like to visit one or more of the neighbouring islands, which are all surprisingly diverse and different . . . .

Martinique This very French island (it's actually a Region of France) is an interesting place to visit with its tropical rain forest, an active volcano (Mt Pelée), fields of pineapples, french/creole cuisine and almost Parisian-style shops. Note: little to no English is spoken.

St Lucia With a size nearly half as big again as Barbados but only half the population, this relatively underpopulated, mountainous and highly forested island makes an interesting contrast to Barbados. Its sulphur springs, military history (the island changed hands 14 times before it became a British colony in 1814), banana plantations and the sight of the majestic Pitons make this a memorable tour. There are two airfields, Hewanorra at the southern tip and Vigie at the capital, Castries. The latter is better for sightseers.

St Vincent St Vincent makes a good starting point for exploring some of the 100 little islands and cays (some uninhabited) that make up the Grenadines. Accommodation rates on St Vincent are still relatively low.

The Grenadines This is the string of little islands between St Vincent and Grenada and includes well-known places like Mustique, Union Island, Bequia and Carriacou. The area is a favourite destination for yachting enthusiasts. In one tour, you fly to the Grenadines then board a schooner for a day's sailing and swimming, before flying home at dusk.

Grenada Known as the "Spice Island" due to the nutmeg, ginger and other spices which are grown for export. With its attractive capital, St George's, and harbour, together with fabulous beaches (including the famous Grand Anse Beach) and forested interior, this pretty island has been a popular tourist destination for many years.

Tobago Part of the state of Trinidad and Tobago, this island can boast deserted beaches and exciting reefs such as the well-known Buccoo Reef off the southern tip. Tobago is also a good place for bird watchers.

You can also arrange to visit places further afield such as Dominica, Margarita and Venezuela.

TRAVEL BY AIR

A one-day tour leaves early in the morning and returns at sunset. Flying time each way is typically an hour. The price is about US$240-285 per person which includes pickup from your hotel, the return flight, a tour of the island and lunch. Alternatively, for about the same price, you can opt for a "two-night" stay where the price includes the return airfare and hotel but excludes meals or island tour. Companies offering these tours are: Caribbean Safari Tours (tel: 427-5100) and Chantours (tel: 432-5591). In addition to the one-day or two-night packages, these tour companies can organise a complete range of trips to meet your requirements. Grenadine Tours (tel: 435-8451) specialise in trips to the Grenadine islands. LIAT, the local island-hopping airline, sometimes offers special airfare bargains that allow you to visit several Caribbean islands at much less than the normal airfare.

TRAVEL BY BOAT

If your budget is more limited, an alternative is to travel by boat to St Lucia or St Vincent. The passenger/cargo ferry, the *Windward* has air-conditioned two-berth cabins and the return fare to St Lucia costs US$99 per person, leaving Friday pm and returning Sunday pm. They also do a 5-night trip to St Vincent for US$199 which includes hotel accommodation. Contact the Windward Lines on tel: 431-0449 or book through Caribbean Safari Tours on tel: 427-5100. Both Caribbean Safari Tours and Chantours (tel: 432-5591) also organise longer, luxury cruises on other vessels ■

SHOPPING, ENTERTAINMENT & EATING

Chapters in this Section:

Jill Walker

SHOPPING

Introduction Barbados has a good variety of shops offering a broad range of local and imported goods. From large department stores and shopping malls to sophisticated boutiques and from supermarkets to mini-marts there is something for every taste, need and budget. Most shops are air-conditioned and well stocked.

Although Barbados is a small island, visitors will discover there is a wide range of attractive products designed or made on the island, such as fashion clothing, swimwear and a huge range of crafts, souvenirs and gifts.

Where are the Shops located? In Bridgetown itself the main shops of interest to visitors are located in and immediately around Broad Street. It is also worth noting that there are some very nice shops out of town where free parking is readily available. For instance:

South Coast: Along this road from town to Dover you can find a range of small boutiques and convenience stores. **Hastings Plaza** and the **Quayside Centre** are shopping arcades and both have a small concentration of interesting shops.

Broad Street, looking west (an unusually quiet moment). The shopping malls of DaCostas (right) and Mall 34 (left) are clearly visible in this picture.

The Quayside Centre at Rockley. An out of town arcade in the popular south side of the island.

St Lawrence Gap: Here you will find convenience stores and small boutiques, in particular **Walkers Caribbean World** that only sells goods made or designed in the Caribbean. There is also the unique **Chattel House Village**, which is a cluster of shops in traditional chattel houses.

Holetown/Sunset Crest: On the west coast there are the two **Sunset Crest Shopping Plazas** (which are shopping centres) together with a number of boutiques in the area.

Speightstown: This has a selection of shops, catering mainly for the local community, and there are some nice shops in the nearby Heywoods Resort.

Parking in Bridgetown Centre Parking can be a problem in the city centre, especially on weekdays, so you may consider coming into town by taxi or bus. If driving, you could use the multistorey car park off Harts Street, which has the added advantage of keeping your car cool. Alternatively you could try the open air car parks at the west end of the Wharf (by Bajan Helicopters) or on the south side of the Careenage in the Independence Square car park. If approached by boys offering to help you park or wash your car, it may be best to decline politely unless you know the ropes.

Shop Opening Hours   Generally, shops open at 8 or 9am and close at 4 or 5pm (supermarkets remain open until later). Most shops close at Saturday lunch-time and are closed on Sundays, except some gift shops located at popular visitor attractions, eg at the Flower Forest, which are open every day.

Methods of Payment   Besides Barbados Dollars, many shops will accept the major credit cards (look for their logos). Shops that cater for tourists will usually also accept US Dollar notes and travellers cheques as the exchange rate with the Barbados Dollar is fixed. Sterling and other currencies are best first changed into Barbados Dollars at a bank or hotel. You will normally get a better rate of exchange at a bank than elsewhere.

BANKS

The main commercial banks are: the Barbados National Bank (tel: 426-0000), Barclays Bank PLC (tel: 431-5151), the Canadian Imperial Bank of Commerce (tel: 431-3700), the Caribbean Commercial Bank (tel: 431-2500), the Mutual Bank of the Caribbean (tel: 436-8335), the Royal Bank of Canada (tel: 426-5200) and Scotiabank (Bank of Nova Scotia) (tel: 431-3000).

All the banks are represented on Broad Street in Bridgetown with branches in the more populated areas such as the south coast and Holetown. Opening hours are normally 8am to 3pm (Monday to Thursday) and 8am to 5pm on Fridays. The Caribbean Commercial Bank also opens on Saturday mornings. The Barbados National Bank's currency exchange booths at the airport and harbour are open every day until the last plane, or cruise ship, leaves.

DUTY FREE SHOPPING

The government has announced major plans which should eventually make Barbados the top duty free centre of the Caribbean. Already today many shops offer duty free shopping to visitors.   Internationally known brands of cameras, china, crystal, electronics, fashion, gems, jewellery, leather goods, knitwear, perfume, shoes, swimwear, television & video equipment and watches are among the goods which are readily available over-the-counter. If you want to purchase rum or other alcohol duty free, then the liquor is delivered to

Duty Free shopping at Cave Shepherd in Broad Street.

the port or airport to be collected by you on your departure.

The department store of **Cave Shepherd**, in Broad Street, is not only the largest department store on the island, but they also have branches at various locations including Sunset Crest (Holetown) and Heywoods and bonded shops at the airport and harbour. Another large store in Broad Street, **Harrisons**, also has duty free shops at the airport and harbour in addition to shops at a number of hotels around the island. In Broad Street or nearby are many other smaller shops offering duty free goods.

Outside Bridgetown, duty free shopping is available at some shops in the **Sunset Crest Shopping Plazas** (Holetown), in many hotel shops and in some of the south coast shops.

For drink and tobacco products remember the duty free shops in the Airport departure lounge when you leave (this is the air-conditioned lounge beyond passport control). This lounge also houses several other duty free shops for your last minute purchases. Do also remember that your own country will have limits on the quantity of duty free goods you can take home.

SHOPPING FOR GIFTS, SOUVENIRS & ANTIQUES

For quality goods to take home as gifts or as pleasing and useful reminders of your holiday, the products stocked in the **Best of Barbados** shops stand out. This is a unique chain of high quality gift shops where everything sold is either designed or made

A small selection of the products available from the Best of Barbados shops.

in Barbados. The shops are well stocked and many items are under Bds$20 (US$10). The work of many Barbadians is represented and the shops feature designs by the talented artist Jill Walker, whose products can also be seen in other shops such as – **Cave Shepherd**, **Harrisons**, **Great Gifts** in DaCostas Mall, the **Mount Gay Rum Visitor Centre** or **Walkers Caribbean World** in St Lawrence. The **Best of Barbados** shops are located at: Andromeda Gardens, Flower Forest, Mall 34 (in Broad St), Passenger Terminal (for cruise ships), Quayside Centre (at Rockley), Sam Lord's Castle, Sandpiper Inn (Holetown) and Southern Palms Hotel (in St Lawrence Gap).

See also "Arts & Crafts" in the chapter BEST THINGS TO SEE & DO for potteries and studios where local products can be purchased.

If you are interested in original local paintings and other works of art, there are several shops and galleries, for instance – **Articrafts** in Broad Street, the **Coffee & Cream Gallery** in St Lawrence Gap, **Finecrafts** in the Chattel House Village, the many little shops clustered in **Pelican Village** on the Princess Alice Highway and the **Verandah Art Gallery** in Broad Street. In addition, a number of talented Barbadian artists and craftspeople can be seen at their studios by appointment.

For antiques, you could try **Antiquaria** on the Spring Garden Highway, **Claradon Antiques** in Pine Road, Belleville, **Greenwich House Antiques** at Trents Hill in St James and **La Galerie Antique** opposite Paynes Bay in St James.

SHOPPING FOR CLOTHES, FASHION & SWIMWEAR

Barbadians dress smartly and with style, so the island has many chic boutiques that can be found in Bridgetown city centre or, in general, near the main hotels along the west and south coasts.

Perhaps not surprisingly there is a good range of swimwear available in the shops.

In addition to stocking well-known imported fashion labels, the shops in Barbados also sell garments designed by several local talented fashion and swim-wear designers. Fabulous hand painted garments are an island speciality with several designers producing everything from loose shirts to elegant evening wear. These local designs are stocked by **Cave Shepherd** and many fashion boutiques.

*Attractive swimwear from **Ripples**, which is beach-wear designed and made locally. Bright tropical colours are very much their hallmark.*

SHOPPING FOR NECESSITIES (Food & Pharmacies)

Barbados has both large supermarkets and small mini-marts so you will never be far from a food store. In addition, fresh fruit, vegetables and fish can be bought from vendors in the markets – but remember then the price may be negotiable. The supermarkets carry an excellent and wide range of foods with familiar brand names mostly imported from North America, New Zealand and Britain.

Generally a shopping basket of food from a supermarket will cost more than a similar basket in North America or Britain due to freight charges and import duties, so if economising, try to buy local produce whenever possible. See the part on "Some Local Foods" in the chapter EATING OUT (& Self Catering).

Large Supermarkets: The largest supermarkets are **JBs Master Mart** at Sargeant's Village and **Big B Supermarket** at the foot of Rendezvous Hill in Worthing. Other big supermarkets convenient for visitors are the **Super Centre** stores at Southern Plaza in Oistins and Sunset Crest in Holetown and **Jordan's Supermarket** in Fitts Village, St James.

Mini-Marts: There are a whole range of these around the island and many stay open until late. Obviously the choice of goods is less than the large supermarkets. Some of the large petrol filling stations also sell food "basics" too, which can be useful if you are driving around the island and need some bread and milk on your way back to your apartment.

Pharmacies (Chemists): Although supermarkets sell a range of non-prescription medical items, there are excellent pharmacies in most areas (see listing in Yellow Pages). They sometimes display the Rx medical symbol. Several are open on Sundays and public holidays ■

TYPICAL SUPERMARKET PRICES

Prices in 1993. Note prices will vary slightly from one shop to the next.

Milk (I litre carton)	Bds$3.05
Bread (Large sliced loaf)	Bds$2.05-2.35
Margarine (250g Flora)	Bds$1.60
Cheese (500g N.Z. Cheddar)	Bds$6.32
Corn Flakes (340g Kellog's)	Bds$7.27
Tea (100 Ty-Phoo Teabags)	Bds$10.79
Coffee (100g Nescafé)	Bds$6.71
Petrol Per litre	Bds$1.64

BRIDGETOWN CENTRE MAP

PLACE INDEX (for the map overpage)

❶ Fishing Harbour (C1)
❷ Mt Gay Rum Visitor Centre (A1)
❸ Jolly Roger & Bajan Queen Cruises (A1)
❹ Cockspur Rum Distillery (off A1)
❺ Kensington Oval Cricket Ground (A1)
❻ Tourist Information office (B1)
❼ Barbados Investment & Dev. Corp. (C1)
❽ Pelican Village (C1)
❾ Princess Alice Bus Terminal (C1)
❿ Main Post Office (C1)
⓫ Cheapside Market (C1)
⓬ St Mary's Church (B1/C1)
⓭ Lower Green Bus Terminal (C1)
⓮ Immigration Department office (C2)
⓯ James Street Methodist Church (B2)
⓰ Eagle Hall Market (A2)
⓱ Carnegie Public Library (B2)
⓲ Supreme Court (B2)
⓳ Registry Office (B2)
⓴ Central Police Station (B2)
㉑ Nicholls Building (B2)
㉒ Screw Dock (C2)
㉓ Synagogue and Jewish Cemetery (B2)
㉔ Montefiore Fountain (B2)
㉕ YMCA (B3)

㉖ YWCA (A2)
㉗ Frank Collymore Hall (B3)
㉘ Central Bank (B3)
㉙ Parliament Buildings (C2)
㉚ Trafalgar Square & Nelson's Statue (C2)
㉛ Chamberlain Bridge & Indep. Arch (C2)
㉜ Fountain Gardens (C2)
㉝ Treasury Building (C3)
㉞ Charles Duncan O'Neale Bridge (C3)
㉟ Fairchild Street Bus Terminal (C3)
㊱ Medford Mahogany Craft Village (A2)
㊲ Bethel Methodist Church (C3)
㊳ Carlisle Bay (C3)
㊴ Fairchild Street Market (C3)
㊵ St Michael's Cathedral (C3)
㊶ Harrison College (B3)
㊷ Queen's Park (B3/C3)
㊸ Helicopter Landing Pad (C2)
㊹ Queen Elizabeth Hospital (C4)
㊺ St Patrick's Cathedral (C3/C4)
㊻ St Michael's School (C4)
㊼ H.M. Prison Glendairy (A4)
㊽ Government House (B4)
㊾ Ronald Tree House,
   (HQ Barbados National Trust) (B4)

STREET INDEX

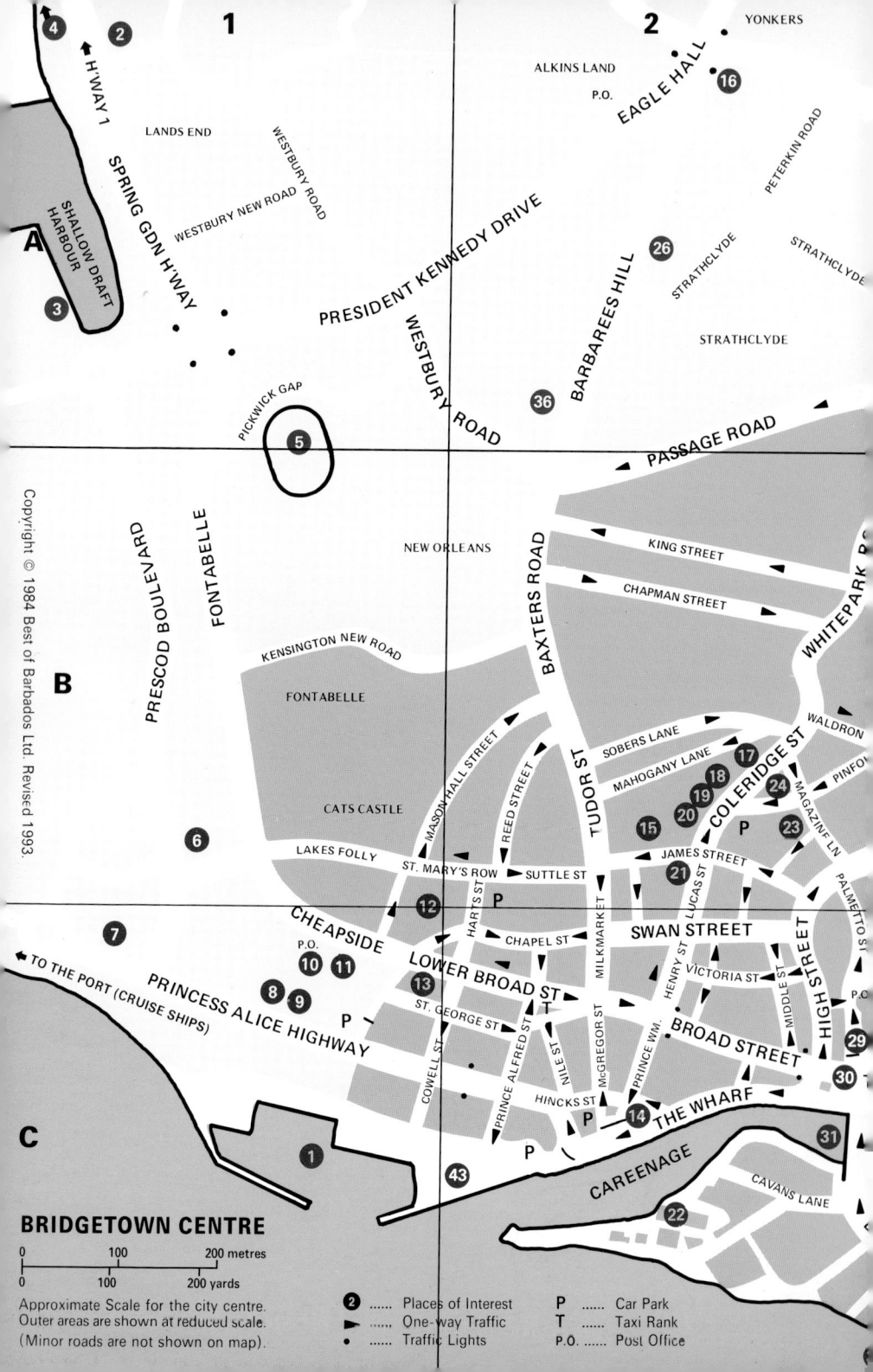

BRIDGETOWN CENTRE

2	Places of Interest
►	One-way Traffic
•	Traffic Lights
P	Car Park
T	Taxi Rank
P.O.	Post Office

0   100   200 metres
0   100   200 yards

Approximate Scale for the city centre.
Outer areas are shown at reduced scale.
(Minor roads are not shown on map).

Copyright © 1984 Best of Barbados Ltd. Revised 1993.

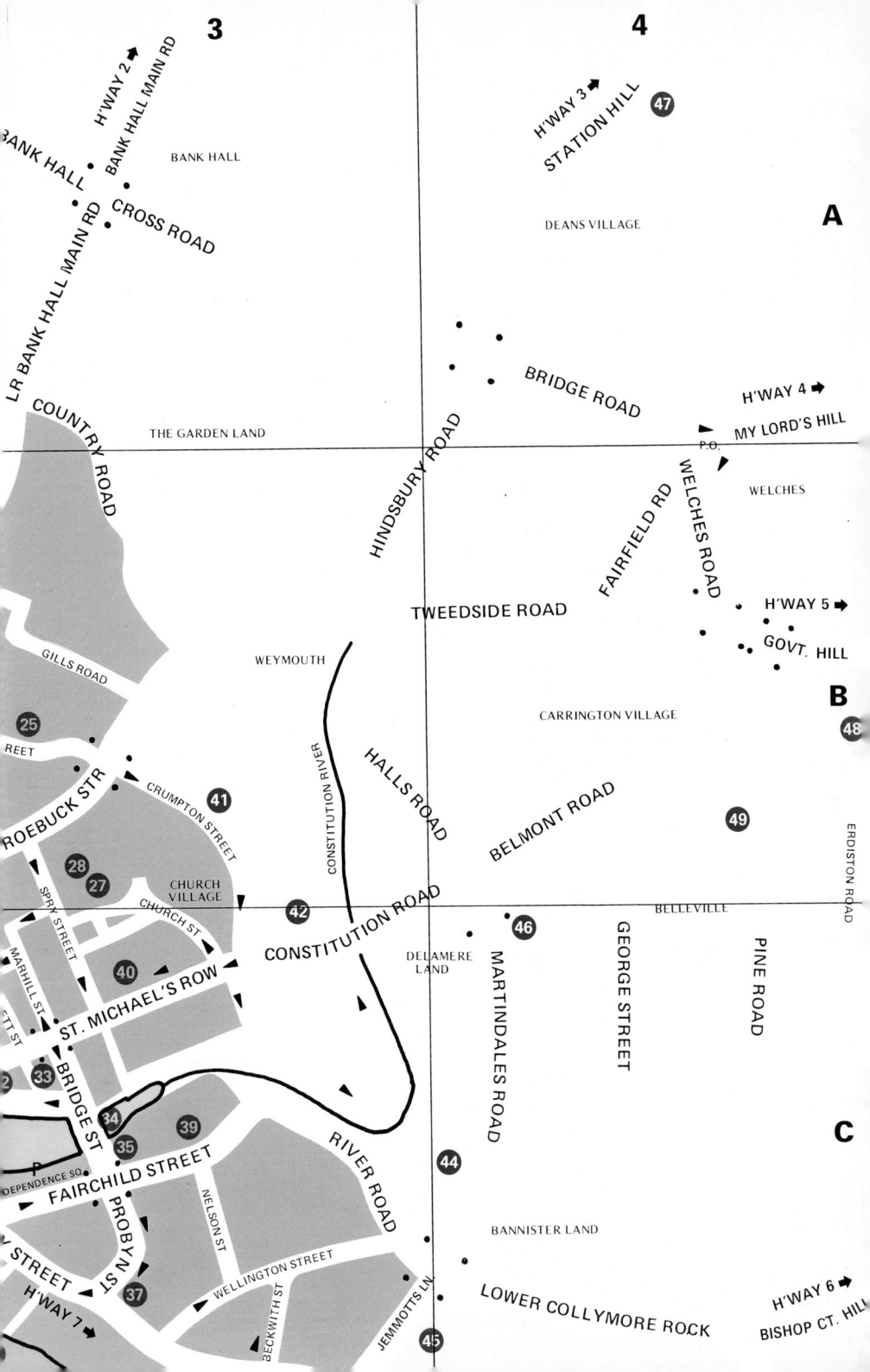

EVENING ENTERTAINMENT

In addition to live bands and floorshows put on at hotels and restaurants on certain evenings of the week, there are some special shows worth seeing . . . .

1627 And All That   As 1627 was the date that the first settlers landed, this show takes place in the appropriate setting of the courtyard of the Barbados Museum. The show takes place every Sunday and Thursday and is a lively, colourful spectacular with folk dancing and singing. A buffet dinner, drinks and tour of the Museum are included in the price, and a steel band plays during intervals and the dinner.   Advance reservations are essential.

The evening show "1627 And All That"

There is a free car park outside the Museum, though transport from/to your hotel is included in the price of Bds$85, which includes drinks, dinner and transport. (Bds$80 if you don't require transport). Telephone: 435-6900.

*Lively entertainment at
The Plantation Garden Theatre.*

Barbados by Night   This is a calypso cabaret show that takes place every Wednesday and Friday night – at The Plantation Restaurant and Garden Theatre. The show features Spice, a very popular local band, and there is also fire eating, limbo dancing and steel band music. A buffet dinner is available and reservations are recommended.

There is car parking available, though transport from/to your hotel is included in the Bds$88 price. The cost just for the Show and drinks is Bds$40 or Bds$88 including dinner and transport. Telephone: 428-5048 or 428-2986.

Plantation Tropical Spectacular   Also at The Plantation Restaurant & Garden Theatre, but on a Monday night, this show lives up to its name – spectacular! Dance to calypso and island music by Emile Straker and the versatile band *No Problem*. Parking, Cost and Telephone – as above.

THEATRES & MUSIC

There is the **Frank Collymore Hall** (a 500-seat Concert Hall situated in the Central Bank Complex) and the **Daphne Joseph-Hackett Theatre** (in Queen's Park). These are the venues for many musical and theatrical performances of interest to both locals and visitors. For details of what's on, look in the free visitor publications, the *SunSeeker* and *Visitor* or the daily newspapers.

Bands The internationally acclaimed Band of the Royal Barbados Police Force plays at a number of events during the year and is well worth hearing. In addition the Band of the Barbados Regiment in their colourful Zouave uniforms are also worth looking out for.

CINEMAS
Although there are a couple of indoor cinemas in Bridgetown, the outdoor "drive-in" cinema will probably appeal most to visitors, especially those from countries where a "drive-in" is a novelty. Films start at sunset and you can take a picnic or buy snacks at the drive-in's snack bar. Forthcoming films are listed in the newspapers. There is currently only the **Globe Drive-in** but at the time of writing a second one was being planned.

BARS
In its long history the island has never been short of watering holes. In his excellent book "Historic Bridgetown", historian Warren Alleyne comments that within a few decades of the first European settlers landing, the town had more than a hundred taverns! Today, there are many places popular with both locals and visitors.

DISCOS & NIGHT-CLUBS
For nightbirds, there are several discos and night-clubs popular with both visitors and locals alike, such as . . . . **After Dark** (St Lawrence Gap); **Club Miliki** (Heywoods Resort); **Club Needhams** (Barbados Hilton Hotel); **Harbour Lights** (Bay Street); **Hippo Disco** (Barbados Beach Village); **The Pepperpot** (St Lawrence Road); **Pier 29** (Cavans Lane) and **The Warehouse** (also Cavans Lane, overlooking the Careenage). The visitor magazine *Ins & Outs of Barbados* will give more details . . . or why not just try them all?

There are no Casinos in Barbados ■

EATING OUT (& SELF CATERING)

Introduction Since Barbados is a major tourist destination catering for many thousands of people, it is no surprise that there is an excellent choice of places to eat. In general, the variety and quality of catering ranges from good to excellent. Barbadians themselves enjoy eating out and you will meet locals in every restaurant.

Prices There is a Government Tax (currently 5%) and menus will usually say if the price already includes the tax. Many restaurants will automatically add a 10% Service Charge. If no service charge is levied, it is normal to tip if you are happy with the service.

LUNCHES & SNACKS

In Bridgetown City Centre: In contrast to many European and North American cities, there are not so many places to eat in the city centre. In addition to the fast food places mentioned below, there are restaurants or snack bars in Cave Shepherd and the shopping Malls of Mall 34, Norman Centre and DaCostas. There is also the **Look Out** on Broad Street and the **Nelson's Arms** in the Galleria Mall opposite Cave Shepherd with an open balcony onto Broad Street. Looking over the Careenage is the **Waterfront Café** and **Fisherman's Wharf**.

Around the island: If you are on an excursion, you will find there are a few places to eat in the rural parts of the island, and many of the attractions have facilities for light refreshments or snacks and these are detailed in the chapters BEST THINGS TO SEE & DO and SIGHTSEEING TOURS. You can also try calling in at one of the many roadside "rum shops" where filled rolls called "cutters" are usually on sale, and there is often baked goodies too, including "rotis" which are hot curried meat pies.

On or near the beach: Most beach front hotels provide light snacks and refreshments and there are a number of beach bars that are popular. Quite a few hotels offer special Sunday buffet lunches.

Fast Food: Barbados has several branches of **Kentucky Fried Chicken, Barbecue Barn** and **Chefette**. For Pizza fans, there are the branches of the **Barbados Pizza House, Pizza-Man-Doc** and **Shakey's Pizza Restaurants**. The food is usually good to very good. (There is no **McDonald's** in Barbados).

EVENING DINING

Excluding small snack bars (called "snackettes"), there are about 200 restaurants in Barbados. Besides the Fast Food outlets listed above, there are restaurants that specialise in Chinese, French, Indian, Italian, seafood or local Bajan dishes. Most hotel restaurants are open to non-residents and some are top class. For homesick English there are pubs such as **The Ship Inn** in St Lawrence Gap and **The Coach House** at Paynes Bay.

The location and ambience of many restaurants are most attractive. For instance **The Schooner** restaurant at Grand Barbados Beach Resort is situated at the end of a 260ft pier jutting into Carlisle Bay. **The Waterfront Café** and **Fisherman's Wharf** overlook the Careenage and Parliament Buildings. Others front onto the beach in a delightful tropical setting. Several are located in old plantation houses. The choice is considerable. For an excellent and comprehensive listing of restaurants with prices and other details, refer to the visitor magazine called *Ins and Outs of Barbados*. Prior booking is usually advisable. Dress depends on the establishment, ranging from completely informal to "smart casual", but beach apparel is not usually acceptable in the evening.

Many restaurants have certain nights when a live band performs, there is dancing or a floor show. See the advertisements in the free visitor publications, the *SunSeeker* and *Visitor*. Sunday lunches too sometimes feature steel bands. Please also refer to the previous chapter in this book EVENING ENTERTAINMENT.

For a completely different dining environment you could choose the Bajan Queen river boat. For details see the entry "Jolly Roger & Bajan Queen Cruises" in the chapter BEST THINGS TO SEE & DO.

SOME LOCAL FOODS (If eating out or cooking for yourself)

You can either eat food you are familiar with or you might like to try some local ones. The fish you are most likely to find on the menu and in the shops are Flying Fish and Dolphin. Flying Fish are about 9 inches (23cm) long and are usually filleted and fried with seasonings. (It is said that if you eat Flying Fish you are sure to return to the island one day!). Dolphin is the local name for a large fish (it's not the porpoise-like mammal), and it is usually served as fish steaks and baked in sauces. You may also find Red Snapper, King Fish (or Wahoo), lobster, octopus, crab-backs, conch and salt fish dishes.

Chicken is a popular dish, often cooked with combinations of fruit like mango, coconut, banana or avocado. Seasoned fried chicken is a national favourite. In fact, spices and seasoning are used quite

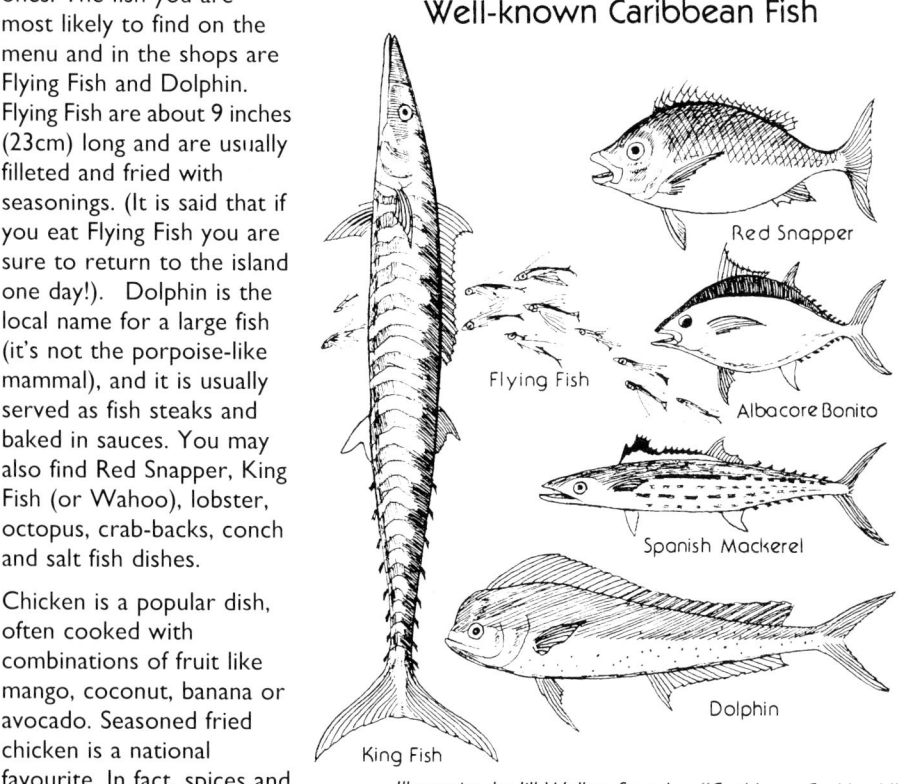

Well-known Caribbean Fish

Red Snapper

Flying Fish

Albacore Bonito

Spanish Mackerel

Dolphin

King Fish

Illustration by Jill Walker from her "Caribbean Cookbook"

liberally in meat dishes. A traditional favourite is Pepperpot, variations of which are found in many southern Caribbean islands. It is essentially a spicy stew of oxtail, pork, beef and chicken with peppers and preserved with cassareep. Pudding and Souse is a haggis-like dish, with well seasoned sweet potato being the basis of the "pudding". This is served sliced with "souse", which is a dish of cold pork and cucumber, seasoned with chopped hot pepper and lime juice. Note that Bajan Hot Pepper sauce is very tasty but is also very hot!

There may be many vegetables new to you. Plantains are like very large bananas but are only eaten cooked. (Visitors can mistake them for bananas when shopping). Plantains are best fried or baked. Breadfruit are large round green "fruit" from the breadfruit tree, brought to the island from the Pacific by Captain Bligh (of *HMS Bounty* fame). Breadfruit are eaten as a vegetable, boiled, baked or fried as chips. Christophene is a pale green pear-shaped vegetable that grows on a vine, and is usually served lightly boiled and occasionally raw in salads. Okras are finger length green vegetables that are usually used

BREAD FRUIT

whole or cross-sectioned in stews, and they are the main ingredient of cou-cou, a traditional dish served with salt fish. Then there are pigeon peas, and eggplant that most visitors will know as aubergine, and there are several shapes of pumpkin, squash and marrow. Root vegetables are grown and eaten widely on the island, including sweet potato, yam, eddoe and tannia.

Depending on the season, local fresh fruits you may find will include: bananas, paw-paw, guavas, mangoes, figs (in this case like a small banana), Barbados cherries (very high in vitamin C), coconuts, soursop, passion fruit, avocados, oranges, grapefruits, sapodillas, carambolas and tamarinds.

If you are cooking for yourself, it may help to have a local cookbook. Have a look at Jill Walker's *Cooking in Barbados* or her *Caribbean Cookbook*. There are many simple and quick recipes using the ingredients that may be new to you. In both books Jill Walker's drawings of island life are a delight. They also depict local fruits and vegetables to help you identify them. Most of the ingredients can be bought in Britain or North America so you can continue with Caribbean cooking when you return home. The books are available from any of the **Best of Barbados** shops ∎

GENERAL INFORMATION

Chapters in this Section:

Introduction Barbados offers the visitor a wide range of accommodation from luxury villa, prestige hotel or resort to more modest hotel or self-catering apartment. Most accommodation is relatively modern and meets North American standards. As a traditional up-market destination there is little accommodation that is mediocre or poor.

The island's hotel building programme is essentially complete, so holidaymakers should not be confronted with the typical building sites so often seen in the Mediterranean. Hotels are generally spaced apart and most are only 2 or 3 storeys high so you never see the ugly high rise, high density type of hotel accommodation that line many beaches elsewhere. Most hotels have their own swimming pools as an alternative to the beach.

Location Most hotels and apartments are spaced along the west coast between Bridgetown and Heywoods (which is the big resort just north of Speightstown), and between Bridgetown and Oistins on the south-western coast. There are a few well-known hotels on the south-eastern coast such as The Crane and Marriott's Sam Lord's Castle. There are no city centre hotels or apartments. Visitor accommodation is mainly sited beside a beach or nearby (usually with just the coast road between it and the beach), but some accommodation is further inland, so check if being very near the beach is important to you.

For visitors wanting to get into Bridgetown or around the island, there are numerous buses and taxis so there is no problem if your hotel is "far" from Bridgetown and if you are self-catering there are usually mini-marts (small supermarkets) nearby.

Seasons The "high season" is generally from mid December to mid April and there can be a considerable difference in accommodation prices between then and the summer "low season". Since the weather does not vary that much, this benefits holidaymakers who wish to visit the island between mid April and mid December.

If you plan to pay for your own hotel accommodation, ie it is not part of a holiday package, then note that you will be charged a Government Tax (currently 5%) and a Service Charge of 10% will usually be added to your hotel bill.

HOTELS & RESORTS

For a complete accommodation list, including the many more modestly priced hotels, contact the Barbados Tourism Authority (see right for addresses) who can provide a leaflet with prices and facilities. Note that prices are quoted in US Dollars per room per day and can vary from as low as US$40 to over US$500.

APARTMENTS

There are many self-catering apartments that can be rented by the week or month. For a complete list, contact the Barbados Tourism Authority who can provide a leaflet with prices, phone numbers and facilities. Note that prices are quoted in US Dollars.

COTTAGES & VILLAS

From modest cottage to grand villa complete with staff and swimming pool, there is a good choice but advance booking is needed especially if you are planning to visit Barbados during the busy Christmas and New Year period. Villas are usually rented out by local Real Estate Agents, such as: Alleyne Aguilar & Altman Ltd at Rose Bank, Derricks, St James (tel: 432-0840); Bajan Services at Seascape Cottage, Gibbs, St Peter (tel: 422-2618); Ronald Stoute & Sons Ltd, Sam Lord's Castle, St Philip (tel: 432-6800); and Realtors Ltd, Riverside House, River Road, St Michael (tel: 426-4900).

Note: The locations of all the larger hotels and apartments are shown on the folded map of Barbados to be found at the end of this book ■

BARBADOS TOURISM AUTHORITY OFFICES

Barbados
P.O. Box 242, Harbour Road, Bridgetown, Barbados.
Tel: (809) 427-2623.   Fax: (809) 426-4080.

Canada
5160 Yonge Street, Suite 1800, North York, Ontario M2N GL19.
Toll Free Tel: 800-268-9122. Fax: (416) 512-6581.
615 Boulevard Dorchester West, Suite 960, Montreal, Quebec H3B 1P5.
Tel: (514) 861-0085.   Fax: (514) 861-7917.

Germany
Rathenau Platz 1A, 6000 Frankfurt a Main.
Tel: 069 28 09 82.   Fax: 069 29 47 82.

United Kingdom
263 Tottenham Court Road, London W1P 9AA.
Tel: 071-636 9448.   Fax: 071-637 1496.

United States
800 Second Avenue, New York, NY 10017.
Toll Free Tel: 800-221-9831.   Fax: (212) 573-9850.

THE BARBADOS HOTEL ASSOCIATION

4th Avenue, Belleville, St Michael, Barbados.
Tel: (809) 426-5041 or (809) 429-7113.   Fax: (809) 429-2845

GENERAL INFORMATION A-Z

EMERGENCY TELEPHONE NUMBERS	Police	112	Police (not Emergency)	436-6600
	Fire	113		
	Ambulance	115	Operator	0

Airlines Barbados has direct scheduled air services with Britain, Europe, the U.S., Canada, Venezuela and the neighbouring Caribbean islands. Approximate flight times to Barbados are: 8½ hours from London (4½ hours by Concorde), 5 hours from Toronto, 4½ hours from New York, 3½ hours from Miami and about 1 hour from nearby islands.

Airport Barbados has one airport – Grantley Adams International, which handles all types of aircraft, including Boeing 747s and Concorde. See also **Departure Tax**.

Auto Rental See **Car Rental**.

Banks For details see the chapter SHOPPING earlier in this book.

Beach Vendors See chapter BEACHES earlier in this book.

Beer The local beer, Banks, has won many international awards. It is a lager which, served chilled, is just right for the tropics. Banks Brewery also produces Carlsberg under licence. Beers brewed in neighbouring islands such as Heineken, Carib, Red Stripe and Ecu can be found on supermarket shelves and in bars. See also **Drinks**.

Bicycle/Scooter Hire Bicycles can be hired by the day (about Bds$25) or week, but note that most roads in Barbados are relatively narrow and the traffic can be quite fast, thereby putting a slow moving bicyclist at risk.

Buses Excluding tour buses (see **Bus Tours**) there are both Transport Board buses (blue with yellow stripe) and private buses (yellow with blue stripe) but all bus fares are a standard Bds$1.50 wherever you travel. Destinations are given on the front of the bus. There are also smaller minibuses with "ROUTE TAXI" signs that ply the bus routes and charge Bds$1.50. To catch a bus, stand at any bus stop sign (a red and white circle) and put your hand out when the bus approaches. In town, you can also catch a bus from the bus terminus at Fairchild Street (for buses to the south and east of the island) or Lower Green (for buses to the west coast and north).

Bus Tours A number of companies run bus tours for visitors, eg L.E. Williams Tours (tel: 427-1043). An all-day island tour costs about Bds$100, including lunch.

Car Parking Generally, parking around the island is not a problem except for the city centre, which is covered in the chapter SHOPPING earlier in this book.

Car Rental A wide range of cars are available for hire. Some have automatic transmission, but most are manual models. Air-conditioning is recommended if you are not used to the heat. You will need a local driving permit (see **Driving**) and ensure you get proper comprehensive vehicle insurance. Rental charges vary quite a bit between operators so it is worth phoning around, but typically will be over Bds$100 per day or between Bds$400-600 per week. Hire companies are listed in the Yellow Pages under "Automobile Renting". See also **Mini-Mokes** below.

Chemists For details see Pharmacies in the chapter SHOPPING.

Churches See **Religious Services**.

Clothing See **Dress Sense**.

Consulates, Embassies & High Commissions For addresses and phone numbers, refer to the Yellow Pages at the back of the Barbados Telephone Directory under "Consulates. . . etc".

Credit Cards Major credit cards are usually accepted but they may not be taken at petrol stations.

Crime See **Security**.

Currency See **Money**.

Dentists For a listing, see the Yellow Pages at the back of the Barbados Telephone Directory. Visitors will need to pay for any dental work.

Departure Tax Every adult leaving the country must pay a departure tax of Bds$25 that will be collected by the airline when checking in.

Doctors Although there is free healthcare for Barbadians, visitors will need to pay for a visit to the Doctor. For a listing, see the Yellow Pages at the back of the Telephone Directory. In an emergency you could visit Casualty at the Queen Elizabeth Hospital.

Dress Sense Barbadians dress well, taking pride in their appearance and expect visitors to do likewise. Beachwear should be reserved for the beach. In shops or while in Bridgetown people are expected to dress more sensibly, ie women should not wear short shorts and men should wear shirts.

Drinking Water The tap water in Barbados is pumped from underground streams and lakes and is of high purity. It is normally safe to drink straight from the tap.

Drinks Spirits and wines are readily available in restaurants and supermarkets but they are quite expensive due to import duties. Soft drinks bottled under licence locally include Coca-Cola, Ju-C, Pepsi, Sprite, Schweppes and 7-Up. Other non-alcoholic drinks include fresh fruit punch, coconut milk and lime juice.

Two less common drinks are Falernum (a rum based liqueur) and Mauby (made by boiling the bark of a small shrub and adding sugar and spices). See also **Beer** and **Rum**.

Driving In Barbados cars drive on the left, as in Britain. In fact British visitors will feel at home with the road signs and regulations though note the speed limits are much lower than in Britain or North America. The maximum speed limit is 50mph (80km/hr) on the Spring Garden Highway and most of the ABC Highway, 37mph (60km/hr) on other country roads and 22mph (35km/hr) in towns. A local driving permit (the Visitors Registration Certificate) is required and should be carried at all times. It costs Bds$10 and is available on production of your own Driving Licence from the Police Stations at Hastings, Holetown and Worthing or through most car rental firms.

Seat belts are not fitted to all cars but with the high density of vehicular traffic on the island's roads, accidents do occur and it's highly advisable to wear seat belts when fitted. In the unfortunate event of an accident, contact the Police and your car rental firm immediately and *do not move* your vehicle until instructed to do so by the Police.

Driving Tips Barbadians are normally polite road users but expect little or very late use of indicators, hence sudden and unexpected manoeuvres by other vehicles. Roads can be very slippery after a rain shower. Some cars may drive very close to your rear or overtake dangerously. As there are no pavements in rural areas, be aware that pedestrians will be using the roads too and are particularly difficult to see at night. Some visitors may be unfamiliar with "roundabouts" – traffic circulates clockwise and you don't enter the roundabout if there is a vehicle coming from your right. On the approach to the roundabout, British drivers please note that lanes are different – left lane for turning left only, right lane for straight on or turning right.

Drugs Drugs of abuse, eg marijuana, are prohibited and there are severe penalties.

Electricity The electrical supply is 110 volts AC, 50Hz (50 cycles) and plugs are standard US design. There are relatively few power cuts, and they don't last long.

Embassies See under **Consulates**. . .

Emergencies See telephone numbers in box at beginning of this A-Z.

Gambling Barbados has no gambling casinos.

Hazards – Natural The island is a relatively safe place. For instance, there are no poisonous snakes but an unlikely meeting with a centipede ("forty legs") can result in a painful bite. Monkeys, if encountered, should also be treated with caution as they too can bite. Lining many beaches are Manchineel trees. Their apple-like fruits are poisonous, and you should not shelter under one if it rains as the washed-down sap can irritate the skin. It is also inadvisable to sit under a coconut tree as a coconut may fall on your head (in fact most hotels remove the coconuts for safety). Probably the greatest hazard is the sun – see **Sunburn** below. See also **Swimming**.

Health Risks Barbados is a remarkably healthy country. There are no prevalent tropical diseases other than Dengue Fever which is spread by mosquitoes and is rare. Mosquito bites can be a nuisance, so take precautions particularly in the evenings, such as burning a mosquito coil. Babies should sleep under mosquito nets. AIDS is becoming a problem as elsewhere in the world.

Hospitals The main hospital is the Queen Elizabeth Hospital, a large General Hospital in Bridgetown. In addition there are several well-equipped private clinics such as the Bayview Hospital.

Hurricanes Although a hurricane is defined as winds over 75mph (120km/hr), gusts can frequently be double that and the destructive force is awesome. Luckily, the location of Barbados to the east of the main chain of islands in the Lesser Antilles helps it to avoid hurricanes. Hurricanes form in the Atlantic and tend to pass to the north of the island before creating havoc in other islands. The main hurricane season is June/July to October/November but in recent years there have been no major hurricanes affecting Barbados (the last being in 1955). The island is however well prepared with hurricane shelters and the paths of hurricanes are plotted by satellite and early warnings are broadcast on TV and radio.

Library The Central Public Library, on Coleridge Street, offers all services to visitors. It is open every day except Sunday. There is also the reference library at the Barbados Museum.

Mail The mail service in Barbados is reliable. You can buy postage stamps from Post Offices and some authorised shops and then post your letters and postcards in the red post boxes, at Post Offices or in the box provided in some hotels. Postal rates change, so you are best to ask when you purchase your stamps. See also Post Offices.

Mini-Mokes   These quaint open-top mini jeeps have been popular with visitors for decades but many of the vehicles are now in poor mechanical condition. Several garages offer new alternative open-top vehicles. If hiring a moke or similar vehicle, remember to use the canopy to reduce sunburn. See also **Car Rental**.

Money   The local currency is the Barbados Dollar. Dollar notes are in denominations of Bds$2,5,10,20,50 and 100. There is also a one dollar silver coin. The Barbados Dollar is linked to the US Dollar at approximately Bds$1 = US 50 cents, but the rate of exchange with Sterling and other countries varies. US dollars are accepted by most stores and hotels, but other currencies less so or not at all.

Newspapers & Magazines   There are currently two daily tabloid newspapers – the *Barbados Advocate* and the *Nation*, both of which have Sunday editions. Two free newspapers aimed at visitors are the *SunSeeker* (twice a month) and the *Visitor* (weekly). Most newsagents also sell British and North American newspapers and magazines, though they may be a few days old.

Parishes   Barbados has eleven parishes and cars registered in the different parishes can be identified by the letter on their number plates: St Lucy (L), St Peter (E), St Andrew (A), St James (S), St Joseph (O), St Thomas (T), St Michael (M), St George (G), St John (J), St Philip (P) and Christ Church (X). Other letters on cars are: a Z on taxis, ZR on "route taxis" and H on hire cars.

Parking   See **Car Parking**.

Pharmacies   For details see the chapter SHOPPING earlier in this book.

Philately   Barbados was one of the earliest countries to issue its own postage stamps (in 1852) and today produces some very attractive stamps which will interest philatelists – there is a Philatelic Bureau at the General Post Office in Cheapside.

Photography   All types of film can be developed and printed quickly on the island by professional photo labs. There are several "one hour" labs in Bridgetown (see under "Photo Finishing" in the Yellow Pages). See also "Photo Tours" on page 63. If you want to take a photograph of someone, it's good manners to ask them first.

Police   See **Security**.

Post Offices   The following Post Offices are located in places convenient to visitors – Cheapside in Bridgetown (the main P.O.) and at Holetown, Speightstown, Oistins and Worthing. Post Offices are open Monday to Friday from 8am to noon, 1pm to 3pm (7am to 5pm at the main P.O.). See also **Mail**.

Public Holidays   These are as follows: New Year's Day (1st January); Errol Barrow's Birthday (21st January); Good Friday and Easter Monday; Labour Day (first Monday in May); Whit Monday; Kadooment (first Monday in August); United Nations Day (first Monday in October); Independence Day (30th November); Christmas Day (25th December) and Boxing Day (26th December).

Radio   See **TV & Radio**.

Religious Services   There are Christian, Jewish, Muslim and Hindu religious services. Refer to a copy of the free newspapers, the *SunSeeker* or *Visitor*, for details.

Route Taxis   See **Buses** and **Taxis**.

Rum   Rum is derived from sugar-cane molasses and is of course the drink most associated with the island. There are two distilleries in Barbados. Rum is often drunk with coke, tonic or in a rum punch or daiquiri (a cocktail). See also **Drinks** and the entry "Rum Tours" in the chapter BEST THINGS TO SEE & DO.

Security   Although Barbados is a tropical paradise, contact with more developed nations and the effects of a recession in the economy have brought about a rise in crime against both locals and visitors. You should therefore take the same sensible precautions as you would take at home, eg always lock your hotel room and hire car. Valuables are best locked in your hotel's safe. Expensive watches, jewellery or money should not be flaunted, and while on the beach keep your possessions close to you. The normally unarmed and helpful Royal Barbados Police can be distinguished by their smart uniform of grey shirt and dark trousers with broad red stripe. If you are in any difficulty, seek help from passing Barbadians who are usually helpful and courteous.

Sunburn   Due to the cooling breezes, visitors may underestimate the sun's strength and the result can be serious sunburn when swimming, sun-bathing or driving around in an open-top car. The answer, of course, is to avoid excessive exposure by keeping out of the sun in the middle of the day, by wearing a good sunblock, T-shirt and sun hat. Watch out too for reflected sunlight near the sea that can burn you even if you are in the shade nearby. If you do get overly sunburnt you could try *aloe vera* – a succulent plant. The yellow juice from a leaf squeezed onto the burn will have a soothing effect. Aloe leaves are often sold by beach vendors at exorbitant prices!

Swimming   For most visitors, a visit to Barbados would be incomplete without swimming in the sea, but see **Hazards-Natural** and **Sunburn** above. Also please refer to the chapter BEACHES earlier in this book where some beaches are listed and there are some *important* safety warnings.

Taxis   There are nearly one thousand taxis in Barbados. They are clearly marked with a "TAXI" sign on the roof and have a "Z" number plate. They can be found outside hotels and in taxi ranks at the airport, the harbour, in Broad Street and Trafalgar Square. Don't confuse these taxis with the small vans that have a "ROUTE TAXI" sign and a "ZR" number plate and which ply the bus routes.

Taxis are not metered so always negotiate a fare before getting in, and check the price is in Barbados, not US, Dollars. A typical fare from the airport to a west coast hotel costs Bds$40-50.

Telephone   Phoning someone else within Barbados is free from private and business phones, but calls are charged from phone booths and most hotel phones. There are excellent direct dialling communications with the rest of the world. The Barbados Telephone Directory gives full details of phone charges and dialling codes. Cellular phones can be rented on a daily basis.

Time Differences   Barbados is 4 hours behind GMT (and 5 hours behind British Summer Time), eg in winter when it's 4pm in Barbados, it's 8pm GMT back in Britain.
Barbados is 1 hour ahead of Eastern Standard Time and is the same during Eastern Daylight Saving Time.

Tipping   Tipping is customary in Barbados if you are satisfied with the service, but note many hotels and restaurants will automatically add a "Service Charge" to the bill.

Tipping (cont'd) Typical tips are: taxis Bds$5-10, hotel maid Bds$20-30 and waiter/waitress 10% of the bill. Tipping is not normal on other occasions.

Tourist Information The Barbados Tourism Authority has an information booth at both the airport and harbour. Their office is on Harbour Road (tel: 427-2623) and is open weekdays during normal office hours. In addition there are two free visitor newspapers, the *Visitor* and the *SunSeeker*, the magazines *Ins & Outs of Barbados* and *Vacation Barbados* and a pocket guide *Barbados In A Nutshell*. These are all excellent sources of information.

TV & Radio Barbados has one colour TV channel (CBC-Caribbean Broadcasting Corporation) but satellite/cable channels are also available. The TV system is North American and not compatible with the European PAL system, so take care when buying a video that it is correct for your own machine. There are also several radio stations in Barbados.

UK Visitor Tips Currently two airlines, British Airways and BWIA, fly direct services from London and there are charter flights from London and Manchester. Some British Airways flights are via Antigua which adds to the journey time, so best avoided if you can. For low price airfares, you could try Caribbean Gold (tel: 081-741 8491) who also do comprehensive package holidays catering for all tastes and budgets. With all tour providers ensure they are ABTA bonded (ATOL if charter). Remember to reconfirm your flight on your return. If you would like to travel to Barbados by sea, the Geest Line (Southampton, tel: 0703 333388) sail their banana boats regularly, but the ship carries few passengers and there is usually a long waiting list of people who want to travel this way (it's not cheap either).

Water See **Drinking Water**.

 If you want to know more about Barbados, there is no better book than the "A-Z of Barbadian Heritage" by Henry Fraser, Sean Carrington, Addinton Forde and John Gilmore. It is packed full of facts and will fascinate both visitors and Barbadians.

INDEX

Note: See also the previous Chapter GENERAL INFORMATION A-Z.

About the Author . . . .

Peter Hingston wrote his first book in 1978 and is now well-known in the UK as an author of guidebooks on small business.

In 1980 he married a Barbadian, Charlotte Walker, and they had a delayed honeymoon in Barbados later that year. He must have found the island attractive and eaten lots of flying fish (which it is reputed will make you revisit Barbados) for in 1981 they returned to live there for several years.

Since 1986 he and his wife have run their own book publishing business. They spend a month or more (as long as possible) in Barbados each year. To write this book required two long "holidays" to revisit the island's many attractions and to complete the necessary research – a most pleasurable task.

Charlotte's parents, Jimmy and Jill Walker, own and run the chain of "Best of Barbados" gift shops and Charlotte's sister and husband, Sue and Chris Trew, also work for "Best of Barbados". The whole family helped with the production of this guidebook, adding their expertise and local knowledge.